Famous Gun Fighters
of the
Western Frontier

DOCK AND THE GAMBLER.

by W. B. (Bat) Masterson

Library of Congress Cataloging-in-Publication Data
Masterson, Bat, 1853-1921.
    Famous gun fighters of the Western Frontier / by W.B. (Bat)
Masterson ; with line drawings by Frederic Remington and others.
      p.   cm.
    Originally published: Golden, CO. : Outbooks, c1986.
    "Ben Thompson, Doc Holliday, Wyatt Earp, Billy Tilghman, Luke
Short, Bat Masterson, and others."
    ISBN 0-89646-087-8
    1. West (U.S.)--Biography. I. Remington, Frederic, 1861-1909.
II. Title.
F591.M1255 1995
978`.02'0922--dc20
    [B]
                                       95-40420
                                           CIP

"HANDS UP!"— THE CAPTURE OF FINNIGAN.

Copyright © 1996 VISTABOOKS
0637 Blue Ridge Road, Silverthorne, CO 80498-8931
ISBN 0-89646-087-8

"DANCE HIGHER—DANCE FASTER."

EDITOR'S PREFACE

Who better than Bat Masterson to write the tales of Ben Thompson, Wyatt Earp, Luke Short, Doc Holliday, Buffalo Bill Cody, and Billy Tilghman—the famous gunfighters of the West? Masterson had lived with, traveled with, and camped with many of his subjects, and had been one of their number, so his accounts are first-person, original history. Besides, he was one of the few who had been both skilled and lucky enough to be left alive in 1907 to write about it.

In that year just after the turn of the century, the editors of *Human Life,* a small and short-lived Boston magazine, wanted to present this earlier period of the Wild American West to their readers, back then a period not so long over. It happened at the time that Masterson was a newspaper reporter in New York, and so they contracted him for the work.

It is somewhat surprising that a man involved so much of his life with more direct forms of communication—the spoken order and the bullet—would also have skills in the written media, but that he had. And so his writing style here is clear as well as full of personal anecdotes. But Bat Masterson would not write about himself—he would write biography, but not autobiography, being modest, the editor explained. Yet his own story had to be included, so the editor wrote it, as part of the "Famous Gunfighters of the Western Frontier"' series but with the special title, "King of the Gunplayers." We present this as the concluding feature.

Many of the illustrations accompanied the original magazine articles; a few by Frederic Remington have been added from another early source, *Century Magazine* for 1888, and still more from other contemporary sources.

Now, read Masterson's tales of the early days when time was too precious and tempers too short for systematic solutions to disputes, but the law of might prevailed—if one only be quick, courageous, and steady enough to win the game! Bat was.

William R. Jones
Series Editor

DRAWN BY MARY HALLOCK FOOTE.

THE SHERIFF'S POSSE.

ENGRAVED BY F. FRENCH.

4

"I FLUNG MYSELF ON HIM."

CONTENTS

"TAKE OFF YOUR BOOTS!"

ON GUARD AT NIGHT.

"Bat" Masterson, 1907
Deputy-Marshal of New York

Introduction
by the Editor of Human Life
January, 1907

WILLIAM BARCLAY (BAT) MASTERSON has been engaged by *Human Life* to write a series of articles on the great old-time gun-players of the West. Mr. Masterson himself is singularly well equipped for the task in hand. He will give us biographical and personal articles on Doc Holliday, Wyatt Earp, Luke Short and others once foremost among this hard-riding, quick-shooting chivalry of the plains. These men were the personal friends of Mr. Masterson. They have slept in his blankets, cooked by his campfire.

Mr. Masterson himself has witnessed stirring times, and stood for years a central and commanding figure in a dangerous day that has gone. His life on the plains began when he was seventeen years old. He has been buffalo hunter, Indian trader, Indian fighter. He was a scout for Miles under the great Ben Clarke—now interpreter at the Cheyenne agency—in the Indian war of 1874. He was in the two weeks' fight at the 'Dobe Walls on the Canadian, when he and thirteen other buffalo hunters fought five hundred of the picked bucks of the Cheyenne, Comanche, Kiowa and Arrapaho tribes, beat them and killed over eighty of them.

Later, at the age of twenty-two, Mr. Masterson was elected sheriff of Ford County, Kansas, with headquarters at Dodge City—an office which, in its duties, covered the sixteen unorganized counties to the west of Dodge City, making a territory three hundred miles east and west by almost as many north and south.

Dodge in that day, was reckoned the roughest camp on the border. It was the northern terminus of the Jones and Plummer trail, over which the beef herds came up from Texas. With them came the cowboys—full of life, vivacity and fight. It took a sure cool hand to keep the peace in Dodge. That Mr. Masterson did not succeed in doing so without a struggle is evidenced by the fact that in the desperate combats of the pistol which ensued, he was driven to kill variously, Walker, Wagner, Kennedy, Updegraffe and King, every one of whom was a "bad man," and had his gun in hand when he fell. But that day is past and Mr. Masterson is no longer a queller of "bad men," but a resident of New York and a contributor to the press. Also he is a warm personal friend of President Roosevelt, who caused him to be named a Deputy United States Marshal for the southern district of New York. President Roosevelt, following his election, was for naming Mr. Masterson marshal in the Indian Territory. The place has twice the salary of the one he holds and carries with it the naming of twenty-two deputies, and yet Mr. Masterson declined it.

"It wouldn't do," he said. "The man of my peculiar reputation couldn't hold such a place without trouble. If I were to go out to the Indian Territory as marshal, I can see what would happen. I'd have some drunken boy to kill once a year. Some kid who was born after I took my guns off would get drunk and look me over; and the longer he looked the less he'd be able to see where my reputation came from. In the end he'd crawl round to a gun play and I'd have to send him over the jump. Almost any other man could hold the office and never see a moment's trouble. But I couldn't; my record would prove a never-failing bait to the dime-novel reading youngsters, locoed to distinguish themselves and make a fire-eating reputation, and I'd have to bump 'em off. So, Mr. President, with all thanks to you, I believe I won't take the place. I've got finally out of that zone of fire and I hope never to go back to it."

It was then President Roosevelt did the next best thing, and caused Mr. Masterson's appointment as a Deputy Marshal in New York.

Julesburg. 1865

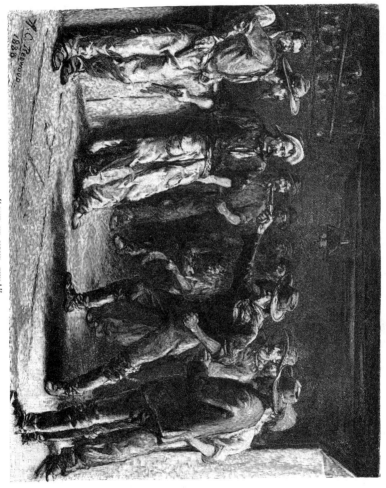

"PUT UP YOUR GUN!"

9

"IT WAS AN ATTITUDE THAT COMMENDED A TEMPORIZING POLICY."

Famous Gun Fighters of the Western Frontier

Ben Thompson

by W. B. (Bat) Masterson

Ben Thompson
A famous "gun fighter" of Texas

I HAVE been asked to write something about the noted killers of men I am supposed to have personally known in the early days of the western frontier and who of their number I regarded as the most courageous and the most expert with the pistol.

In making this request, I may reasonably assume the editor did not consider that he was imposing on me very much of a task, and had it embodied nothing more than the question of proficiency with the pistol, such would have been the case; but in asking me to offer an opinion on the question of physical courage as sometimes exemplified by them under nerve-trying conditions, he has placed a responsibility on my shoulders that I hardly care to assume. I have known so many courageous men in that vast territory lying west and south-west of the Missouri River—men who would when called upon face death with utter indifference as to consequences, that it would be manifestly unjust for me even to attempt to draw a comparison.

Courage to step out and fight to the death with a pistol is but one of three qualities a man must possess in order to last very long in this hazardous business. A man may possess the greatest amount of courage possible and still be a pathetic failure as a "gun fighter," as men are often called in the West who have gained reputations as "man-killers." Courage is of little use to a man who essays to arbitrate a difference with the pistol if he is inexperienced in the use of the weapon he is going to use. Then again he may possess both courage and experience and still fail if he lacks deliberation.

Any man who does not possess courage, proficiency in the use of fire-arms, and deliberation had better make up his mind at the beginning to settle his personal differences in some other manner than by an appeal to the pistol. I have known men in the West whose courage could not be questioned and whose expertness with the pistol was simply marvelous, who fell easy victims before men who added deliberation to the other two qualities. I will cite a few such instances that came under my own personal observation.

The Harrison-Levy Feud

Thirty-five years ago Charlie Harrison was one of the best-known sporting men west of the Missouri River. His home was in St. Louis but he traveled extensively throughout the West and was well-known through the Rocky Mountain region. He was of an impetuous temperament, quick of action, of unquestioned courage and the most expert man I ever saw with a pistol. He could shoot faster and straighter when shooting at a target than any man I ever knew; then add to that the fact that no man possessed more courage than he did, the natural conclusion would be that he would be a most formidable foe to encounter in a pistol duel.

In 1876 he started for the Black Hills, which was then having a great mining boom on account of the discovery of gold at Deadwood. When Charley reached Cheyenne he became involved in a personal difficulty with another gambler by the name of Jim Levy, and both men started for their respective lodgings to get their pistols and have it out the first time they met. It looked like 100 to 1 that Harrison would win the fight because of his well-known courage and proficiency in the use of the pistol. Little being known at that time about Jim Levy, Harrison was made a hot favorite in the betting in the various gambling resorts of Cheyenne. The men were not long in getting together after securing their revolvers, which were of the Colts pattern and of 45 calibre in size.

They met on opposite sides of the principal street of the city and opened fire on each other without a moment's delay. Harrison, as was expected, fairly set his pistol on fire, he was shooting so fast and managed to fire five shots at Levy before the latter could draw a bead on him. Levy finally let go a shot. It was all that was necessary. Harrison tumbled into the street in a dying condition and was soon afterwards laid to rest alongside of others who had gone before in a similar way.

That Harrison was as game a man as Levy could not be doubted; that he could shoot much faster, he had given ample proof, but under extraordinary conditions he had shown that he lacked deliberation and lost his life in consequence. The trouble with Charley Harrison was just this—he was too anxious. He wanted to shoot too fast. Levy took his time. He looked through the sights on his pistol, which is a very essential thing to do when shooting at an adversary who is returning your fire.

Johnny Sherman, another well-known Western sport and a near relative of the famous Sherman family of Ohio, was another remarkably fine pistol shot. When he happened to be where he could not go out and practice with his pistol, he would hunt up a shooting gallery and spend an hour or so practicing with the gallery pistols.

"ARE YOU SATISFIED?"

13

Wanted to Shoot too Fast

In this way he became an adept in the use of the revolver. He was, as everyone who knew him can testify to, as courageous as a lion and yet, when he started in to kill a dentist in a room in a St. Louis hotel, who had, as he claimed, insulted his wife, he emptied his pistol at the dentist without as much as puncturing his clothes, and mind you, the dentist was not returning his fire. Sherman, like Harrison, was in too big a hurry to finish the job and forgot that there were a set of sights on his pistol.

Levie Richardson is another case in point that will serve to show that coolness and deliberation are very essential qualities in a shooting scrape, and unless a man possesses them, he is very apt to fall a victim to the man who does. Levie Richardson had been a buffalo hunter with me on the plains of western Kansas for several years. We were very close friends and shared our blankets with each other on a great many cold winter nights, when blankets were a very useful commodity. He was thoroughly familiar with the use of fire-arms and an excellent shot with either pistol or rifle. He was a high-strung fellow who was not afraid of any man. He got a notion into his head one night in Dodge City, Kansas, that a young gambler by the name of Frank Loving, generally known as "Cock-eyed Frank," had done him some wrong, and forthwith made up his mind to kill him on sight. He publicly declared what he intended to do to Loving as soon as he met him, and some busybody who had been listening to the threats hastened away to put Loving on his guard.

Frank Loving was a mere boy at the time, but he was not afraid and immediately proceeded to arm himself and be prepared to deal out the best that he had when his man came. He did not have to wait very long, for Richardson was a man to act promptly when once he had made up his mind to do a certain thing; and as he had decided on killing Loving with as little delay as possible, the battle was on almost before a person had time to think. Richardson found Loving sitting unconcernedly on a card table in the Long Branch Saloon and instantly opened fire on him with his Colts 45 calibre pistol. He fired five times at his man in rapid succession, but missed with every shot, and was finally shot dead by Loving, who took his time about his work. It was the cleanest possible shot.

Richardson, like Harrison and Sherman, did not take sufficient time to see what he was doing and his life paid the penalty. No one, however, who know both men could truthfully say that Loving possessed a greater degree of courage than Richardson, or that under ordinary conditions he was a better marksman with a gun. He simply had the best nerve, which is a quality quite different from courage. Courage, generally speaking, is daring.

Nerve is steadiness.

I was the sheriff of the county at the time and refused to lock Loving up in jail, holding that he had, in killing Richardson, only acted in self defense; and permitted him to be at large on his own recognizance until his preliminary examination was held, which exonerated him, as I knew it would. I have never stood for murder and never will, but I firmly believe that a man who kills another in defense of his own life should always be held blameless and will always lend a helping hand to such a man.

14

Frank Loving was himself murdered three years later by another gambler by the name of John Allen, in Trinidad, Colorado. Allen, soon after his acquittal for the murder of Loving, became a street preacher and of course all has been forgiven.

The Career of Ben Thompson

But all this is preliminary to the real purpose of this story, which is to tell something about Ben Thompson, the famous "gun fighter" of Austin, Texas. Ben Thompson was born in England and came to this country with his family when a boy. The family settled in Austin, Texas, and Ben learned the printer's trade and set type in the local newspaper offices of the city.

When the Civil War broke out he enlisted as a private in one of the Texas regiments and went to the front to fight the battles of the lost cause. He was only a boy in years when he enlisted, but was not long in showing the kind of mettle that was in him. While serving in General Kirby Smith's command during the campaign along the Red River, young Thompson performed many deeds of great daring, such as crossing into the enemy's lines and in carrying important despatches for the officers of his command. For the dash and courage he displayed at the battle of Sabine Cross Roads, just above the mouth of Red River in Louisiana, he was promoted to the rank of captain by his commanding officer. At the conclusion of hostilities between the North and South Ben returned to his home in Austin, but did not remain long. The spirit of war was now upon him and he longed for more conflict.

Austin was too peacefully disposed for him, so he immediately set out for old Mexico, where Maximilian was just then having a lively time maintaining himself in his position as Emperor of Mexico. After getting on Mexican soil Ben lost no time in reaching the headquarters of Maximilian's army, where he tendered his services in behalf of the invader's cause. He was instantly accepted and commissioned a captain and was soon wearing the uniform of the Emperor's army. Ben, however, was not given much opportunity to achieve distinction in the invading army, for Maxmilian soon after suffered a collapse and Thompson was lucky to get away from the Mexicans and reach his home in Austin with his life.

Ben Thompson was a remarkable man in many ways and it is very doubtful if in his time there was another man living who equalled him with the pistol in a life and death struggle. Thompson in the first place possessed a much higher order of intelligence than the average "gun fighter" or man killer of his time.

He was more resourceful and a better general under trying conditions than any of that great army of desperate men who flourished on our frontier thirty years ago. He was absolutely without fear and his nerves were those of the finest steel. He shot at an adversary with the same precision and deliberation that he shot at a target. He was a past master in the use of the pistol and his aim was as true as his nerves were strong and steady. He had during his career more deadly encounters with the pistol than any man living and won out in every single instance. The very name of Ben Thompson was enough to cause the general run of "man killers," even those who had never seen him, to seek safety in instant flight. Thompson killed many men during his career, but

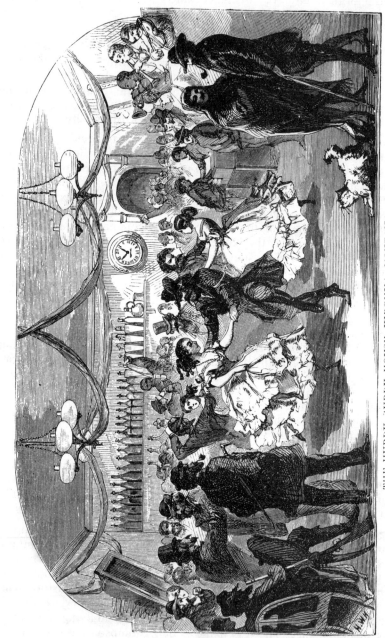

THE HURDY-GURDY HOUSE, VIRGINIA, MONTANA.

always in an open and manly way. He scorned the man who was known to have committed murder, and looked with contempt on the man who sought for unfair advantages in a fight.

The men whom he shot and killed were without exception men who had tried to kill him; and an unarmed man or one who was known to be a non-combatant, was far safer in his company than he would be right here on Broadway at this time. He was what could be properly termed a thoroughly game man, and like all men of that sort never committed murder. He stood about five feet nine inches in height and weighed in later years, in the neighborhood of 180 pounds.

Wore Silk Hat and Prince Albert

His face was pleasant to look upon and his head was round and well-shaped. He was what could be called a handsome man. He was always neat in his dress but never loud, and wore little if any jewelry at any time. He was often seen on the streets of Austin, especially on a Sunday, wearing a silk hat and dressed in a Prince Albert suit of the finest material. While he was not given to taking any unnecessary chances with his life, he would unhesitatingly do so if he felt that occasion demanded it. For example:

He had a falling out one day with the proprietor of a vaudeville house in Austin and that night, just at the busiest hour, went over to the place and fired a shot from his pistol into one of the big chandeliers that was hanging from the ceiling, which broke some of the glass shades and scattered the pieces of broken glass in all directions over the audience. This, as might be expected, caused an immediate stampede of the patrons who rushed pell mell for the street. Thompson, when things quieted down somewhat, left the place without offering to do any further mischief. That seemed to satisfy Ben and in all probability the trouble would have ended then and there had the proprietor let the matter rest where it was; but he refused to listen to the advice of his friends and openly declared that he intended to get even with Thompson. As a matter of course everything he said about Ben was instantly carried to him and, as is generally the way in such cases, some things he did not say were added to the story by the tale-bearers.

The Threat of the Vaudeville Man

At any rate it got noised about town that the vaudeville man was thoroughly organized for Ben and intended to kill him the first time he ever stepped inside his house. Of course Ben was told what was being said about him by the hurdy-gurdy manager, but only laughed and said that he guessed if he didn't die until he got killed by the showman, he would live a long time. But reports of the threats that were being made against his life by the vaudeville proprietor kept reaching him with such regularity, that he finally began to think that perhaps there might be something in them. At any rate he made up his mind to see for himself how much there really was in those threats that he had been hearing about for so long. So one night while the show was in full blast he told a very warm personal friend of his by the name of Zeno Hemphill that he had made up his mind to go over to the show and look over the arrangements he understood had been made for his removal from this vale of tears.

17

"Zeno," said Ben "just fall in a few feet behind me and 'holler' if you see anything that doesn't look exactly right to you when I get inside that 'Honkitonk.' "Remember, Zeno, I only want you along for a witness in case anything happens," remarked Ben, as he started to cross the street to the variety theater that was soon to witness a terrible tragedy within its walls. Ben entered a door that led to the bar-room from the street. This bar-room was a part of the theater, although the stage upon which the performance appeared was in another part of the building.

In order to reach that part of the building in which a performance was being given it was necessary for Ben to pass along the entire length of the bar, then through a pair of swinging doors located about ten feet further on, through which it was necessary to pass before a view of the stage could be obtained. When Ben first entered the bar-room he took a hasty survey of the surroundings but saw nothing to cause alarm. In fact he did not expect the attack to come from that part of the house, if indeed an attack was made at all, but was looking for it to occur after he had reached the theatre proper, which would not be until after he had passed the swinging doors. Ben did not stop in the bar-room but kept on walking leisurely towards the swinging doors and just as he was about to push them apart he heard Zeno, who had just then stepped into the room, cry out, "Look out, Ben." But before Ben could scarcely move, the bartender, whose name was Mark Wilson, had raised a double-barrelled shot gun that he had lying along the mixing board back of the bar, and

A ROW IN A CATTLE TOWN.

18

emptied both barrels, which were heavily loaded with buckshot, at Ben, who could not have been more than ten feet away.

Incredible as it may seem Thompson escaped without a scratch. Mark Wilson, the bartender, was known to be a courageous young fellow who had on several occasions shown considerable fighting grit, and for that reason he had been selected to kill Thompson the first time he entered the place. Wilson, however, realizing that he was taking upon himself something of a job in agreeing to dispose of Ben Thompson, concluded that it would be best to get a little help, so he went to his friend Sam Mathews, and told him what he had made up his mind to do and asked him if he would help him out in the matter.

"With great pleasure," replied Mathews, and straightway went for his trusty Winchester rifle and immediately repaired to the variety theatre to help out his friend Wilson in putting Ben Thompson out of the way.

When Ben entered the bar-room that evening he saw Mathews standing around the corner of the bar, but did not notice that he had a Winchester rifle leaning by his side; in fact did not regard Mathews, whom he know quite well, as an enemy and perhaps for that reason did not look him over very carefully. But to get to the point. The smoke from the shot gun had scarcely blown aside before Ben had whipped out his pistol and like a flash of lightning had shot Wilson dead in his tracks. Ben then noticed that Mathews had a Winchester rifle in his hand and instantly concluded that he too, was there for the purpose of aiding Wilson in killing him. Mathews seemed to anticipate what was passing through Thompson's mind, for he ducked down behind the bar instead of attempting to use the rifle. Thompson, instead of going around the end of the bar where he could see Mathews, took a rough guess at his location and fired through the end of the bar. The bullet struck Mathews squarely in the mouth and toppled him over on the floor.

When Case Was Called for Trial

Ben then turned around and walked out of the place with his friend, Zeno Hemphill, who later on when the case was called for trial, was the most important witness for the defence. Ben was kept locked up in jail pending the preliminary examination and was then admitted to bail and subsequently acquitted.

This is only one of a dozen of such occurrences that could be cited in the career of this most remarkable man. Wilson and Mathews were unquestionably men of courage, else they could not have been induced to enter into a plot to kill such a desperate man as they knew Thompson to be; but when it came to the scratch they both lost their nerve and Ben was privileged to add two more names to the list of ambitious "gun fighters," who had sought to take his life. Thompson served a term as chief of police of the city of Austin and all the old-time citizens of the place remember him still as the best chief of police the city ever had. While Thompson was known throughout all that vast territory lying west and south-west of the Missouri River as the nerviest of men, and as unerring a shot with a pistol as ever lived; there were several men contemporaneous with himself who had the occasion arisen, would have given him battle to the death.

All with Nerves of Steel

Such men as "Wild Bill" Hickok, Wyatt Earp, Billy Tilghman, Charley Bassett, Luke Short, Clay Allison, Joe Lowe and Jim Curry were all men with nerves of steel who had often been put to the test—any one of whom would not have hesitated a moment to put up his life as the stake to be played for. Those men, all of them, lived and played their part and played it exceeding well on the lurid edge of our Western frontier at the time Ben Thompson was playing his, and it is safe to assume that not one of them would have declined the gage of battle with him had he flung it down to any one of their number.

In making this admission, however, I am constrained to say that little doubt exists in my mind but that Thompson would have been returned the winner of the contest. Ben Thompson was murdered along with his personal friend, King Fisher, in a vaudeville theatre in San Antonio, Texas, in March, 1884.

Both he and King Fisher were killed from ambush by a number of persons who were concealed in the wings of the stage, and neither ever knew what happened. Ben was hit eight times by bullets fired from a Winchester rifle, and King Fisher was hit five times. All the shots were fired simultaneously and both sank to the floor dead as it is possible to ever be. It was a cold-blooded, cruel and premeditated murder, for which no one was ever punished by law.

WILD BILL.

HOME FOR THE BOYS.

21

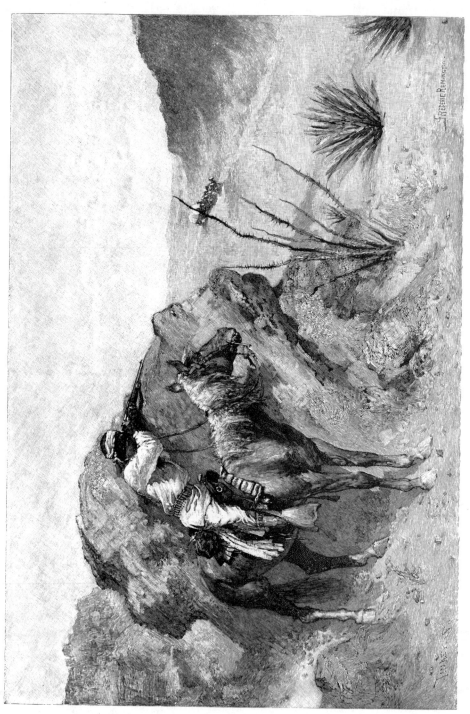

AN APACHE INDIAN.

22

Famous Gun Fighters of the Western Frontier

Wyatt Earp

by W. B. (Bat) Masterson

Wyatt Earp
Well-known throughout Kansas in the seventies as Marshal of Dodge City, and a man who never showed the white feather.

THIRTY-FIVE years ago that immense stretch of territory extending from the Missouri River west to the Pacific Ocean, and from the Brazos River in Texas north to the Red Cloud Agency in Dakota, knew no braver nor more desperate man than Wyatt Earp, the subject of this narrative.

Wyatt Earp is one of the few men I personally knew in the West in the early days, whom I regarded as absolutely destitute of physical fear. I have often remarked, and I am not alone in my conclusions, that what goes for courage in a man is generally the fear of what others will think of him—in other words, personal bravery is largely made up of self-respect, egotism, and an apprehension of the opinion of others.

Wyatt Earp's daring and apparent recklessness in time of danger is wholly characteristic; personal fear doesn't enter into the equation, and when everything is said and done, I believe he values his own opinion of himself more than that of others, and it is his own good report that he seeks to preserve. I may here cite an incident in his career that seems to me will go far toward establishing the correctness of the estimate I have made of him.

Claimed the Cards were Crooked

He was once engaged in running a faro game in Gunnison, Colorado, in the early days of that camp; and one day while away from the gambling house, another gambler by the name of Ike Morris, who had something of a local reputation as a bad man with a gun, and who was also running a faro game in another house in the camp, went into Wyatt's game and put down a roll of bills on one of the cards and told the dealer to turn. The dealer did as he was told, and after making a turn or two, won the bet and reached out on the layout and picked up the roll of bills and deposited them in the money-drawer. Morris instantly made a kick and claimed that the cards were crooked, and demanded the return of his money. The dealer said that he could not give back the money, as he was only working for wages, but advised him to wait until Mr. Earp returned, and then explain matters to him, and as he was the proprietor of the game he would perhaps straighten the matter up. In a little while Wyatt returned, and Morris was on hand to tell him about the squabble with the dealer, and incidentally ask for the return of the money he had bet and lost.

Wyatt told him to wait a minute and he would speak to the dealer about it; if things were as he represented he would see what could be done about it. Wyatt stepped over to the dealer and asked him about the trouble with Morris. The dealer explained the matter, and assured Wyatt that there was nothing wrong with the cards, and that Morris had lost his money fairly and squarely. By this time the house was pretty well filled up, as it got noised about that Morris and Earp were likely to have trouble. A crowd had gathered in anticipation of seeing a little fun. Wyatt went over to where Morris was standing and stated that the dealer had admitted cheating him out of his money, and that he felt very much like returning it on that account; but said Wyatt—"You are looked upon in this part of the country as a bad man, and if I was to give you back your money you would say as soon as I left town, that you made me do it, and for that reason I will keep the money." Morris said no more about the matter, and after inviting Wyatt to have a cigar, returned to his own house, and in a day or so left the camp.

Lost his Reputation in the Camp

There was really no reason why he should have gone away, for so far as Wyatt was concerned the incident was closed; but he perhaps felt that he had lost whatever prestige his reputation as a bad man had given him in the camp, and concluded it would be best for him to move out before some other person of lesser note than Wyatt Earp took a fall out of him. This he knew would be almost sure to happen if he remained. He did not need to be told that if he remained in town after the Earp incident got noised about, every Tom, Dick and Harry in camp would be anxious to take a kick at him, and that was perhaps the reason for his sudden departure for other fields where the fact of his punctured reputation was not so generally known.

The course pursued by Earp on this occasion was undoubtedly the proper one—in fact the only one—able to preserve his reputation and self-respect. It would not have been necessary for him to have killed Morris in order to have sustained his reputation, and very likely that was the very last thing he had in mind at the time, for he was not one of those human tigers who delighted in shedding blood just for the fun of the thing. He never, at any time in his career, resorted to the pistol excepting in cases where such a course was absolutely necessary. Wyatt could scrap with his fists, and had often taken all the fight out of bad men, as they were called, with no other weapons than those provided by Nature.

There were few men in the West who could whip Earp in a rough-and-tumble fight thirty years ago, and I suspect that he could give a tough youngster a hard tussle right now, even if he is sixty-one years of age. In all probability had Morris been known as a peaceable citizen, he would have had his money returned when he asked for it, as Wyatt never cared much for money; but being known as a man with a reputation as a gun-fighter, his only chance to get his money back lay in his ability to "do" Earp, and that was a job he did not care to tackle.

I have known Wyatt Earp since early in the seventies, and have seen him tried out under circumstances which made the test of manhood supreme. He landed in Wichita, Kansas, in 1872, being then about twenty-six years old, and weighing in the neighborhood of one hundred and sixty pounds, all of it muscle. He stood six feet in height, with light blue eyes, and a complexion bordering on the blonde. He was born at Monmouth, Illinois, of a clean strain of American breeding, and served in an Iowa regiment the last three years of the Civil War, although he was only a boy at the time. He always arrayed himself on the side of law and order, and on a great many occasions, at the risk of his life, rendered valuable service in upholding the majesty of the law in those communities in which he lived. In the spring of 1876 he was appointed Assistant City Marshal of Dodge City, Kansas, which was then the largest shipping point in the North for the immense herds of Texas cattle that were annually driven from Texas to the northern markets. Wyatt's reputation for courage and coolness was well known to many of the citizens of Dodge City—in fact it was his reputation that secured for him the appointment of Assistant City Marshal.

He was not very long on the force before one of the alderman of the city, presuming somewhat on the authority his position gave him over a police-officer, ordered Wyatt one night to perform some official act that did not look exactly right to him, and Wyatt refused point blank to obey the order. The alderman, regarded as something of a scrapper himself, walked up to Wyatt and attempted to tear his official shield from his vest front where it was pinned. When that alderman woke up he was a greatly changed man. Wyatt knocked him down as soon as he laid his hands on him, and then reached down and picked him up with one hand and slammed a few hooks and upper-cuts into his face, dragged his limp form over to the city calaboose, and chucked it in one of the cells, just the same as he would any other disturber of the peace. The alderman's friends tried to get him out on bail during the night, but Wyatt gave it out that it was the calaboose for the alderman until the police court opened up for business at nine o'clock the following morning, and it was. Wyatt was never bothered any more while he lived in Dodge City by aldermen.

While he invariably went armed, he seldom had occasion to do any shooting in Dodge City, and only once do I now recall when he shot to kill, and that was at a drunken cow-boy, who rode up to a Variety Theatre where Eddie Foy, the now famous comedian, was playing an engagement. The cow-boy rode right by Wyatt, who was standing outside the main entrance to the show shop, but evidently he did not notice him else he would not in all probability have acted as he did.

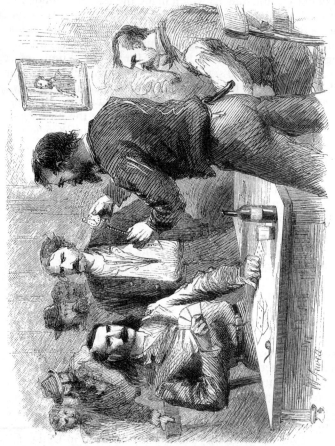

PUTTING UPON HIM.

An Incident not on the Program

The building in which the show was being given was one of those pine-board affairs that were in general use in frontier towns. A bullet fired from a Colts 45 calibre pistol would go through a half-dozen such buildings, and this the cow-boy knew. Whether it was Foy's act that angered him, or whether he had been jilted by one of the chorus we never learned; at any rate he commenced bombarding the side of the building directly opposite the stage upon which Eddy Foy was at that very moment reciting that beautifully pathetic poem entitled "Kalamazoo in Michigan", The bullets tore through the side of the building scattering pieces of the splintered pine-boards in all directions. Foy evidently thought the cow-boy was after him, for he did not tarry long in the line of fire. The cow-boy succeeded in firing three shots before Wyatt got his pistol in action. Wyatt missed at the first shot, which was probably due to the fact that the horse the cow-boy was riding kept continually plunging around, which made it rather a hard matter to get a bead on him. His second shot, however, did the work, and the cow-boy rolled off his horse and was dead by the time the crowd reached him.

Wyatt's career in and around Tombstone, Arizona, in the early days of that bustling mining camp was perhaps the most thrilling and exciting of any he ever experienced in the thirty-five years he has lived on the lurid edge of civilization. He had four brothers besides himself who waggoned it into Tombstone as soon as it had been announced that gold had been discovered in the camp.

Jim was the oldest of the brothers. Virgil came next, then Wyatt, then Morgan, and Warren, who was the kid of the family. Jim started in running a saloon as soon as one was built. Virgil was holding the position of Deputy U.S. Marshal. Wyatt operated a gambling house, and Morgan rode as a Wells Fargo shot-gun messenger on the coach that ran between Tombstone and Benson, which was the nearest railroad point. Morgan's duty was to protect the Wells Fargo coach from the stage robbers with which the country at that time was infested.

Stage Robbers of San Simon Valley

The Earps and the stage robbers knew each other personally, and it was on this account that Morgan had been selected to guard the treasure the coach carried. The Wells Fargo Company believed that so long as it kept one of the Earp boys on the coach their property was safe; and it was, for no coach was ever held up in that country upon which one of the Earp boys rode as guard.

A certain band of those stage robbers who lived in the San Simon Valley, about fifty miles from Tombstone and very near the line of Old Mexico, where they invariably took refuge when hard pressed by the authorities on the American side of the line, was made up of the Clanton borthers, Ike and Billy, and the McLowry brothers, Tom and Frank. This was truly a quartette of desperate men, against whom the civil authorities of that section of the country at that time were powerless to act. Indeed, the United States troops from the surrounding posts, who had been sent out to capture them dead or alive, had on more than one occasion returned to their posts after having met with both failure and disaster at the hands of the desperadoes.

Those were the men who had made up their minds to hold up and rob the Tombstone coach; but in order to do so with as little friction as possible, they must first get rid of Morgan Earp. They could, as a matter of course, ambush him and shoot him dead from the coach; but that course would hardly do, as it would be sure to bring on a fight with the other members of the Earp family and their friends, of whom they had a great many. They finally concluded to try diplomacy. They sent word to Morgan to leave the employ of the Wells Fargo Express Company, as they intended to hold up the stage upon which he acted as guard, but didn't want to do it as long as the coach was in his charge. Morgan sent back word that he would not quit and that they had better not try to hold him up or there would be trouble. They then sent word to Wyatt to have him induce Morgan, if such a thing was possible, to quit his job, as they had fully determined on holding up the coach and killing Morgan if it became necessary in order to carry out their purpose.

Wyatt sent them back word that if Morgan was determined to continue riding as guard for Wells Fargo he would not interfere with him in any way, and that if they killed him he would hunt them down and kill the last one in the bunch. Just to show the desperate character of those men, they sent Virgil Earp, who was City Marshal of Tombstone at the time, word that on a certain day they would be in town prepared to give him and his brothers a battle to the death. Sure enough, on the day named Ike and Billy Clanton and Tom and Frank McLowry rode into Tombstone and put their horses up in one of the city corrals. They were in town some little time before the Earps knew it. They never suspected for a moment that the Clantons and McLowrys had any intention of carrying out their threat when they made it. When Virgil Earp fully realized that they were in town he got very busy. He knew that it meant a fight and was not long in hustling up Wyatt and Morgan and ''Doc'' Holliday, the latter as desperate a man in a tight place as the West ever knew. This made the Marshal's party consist of the Marshal himself, his brothers Wyatt and Morgan, and ''Doc'' Holliday. Against them were the two Clantons and the two McLowrys, an even thing so far as numbers were concerned. As soon as Virgil Earp got his party together, he started for the corral, where he understood the enemy was entrenched, prepared to resist to the death the anticipated attack of the Earp forces.

The Town Turned out for the Battle

Everybody in Tombstone seemed to realize that a bloody battle was about to be fought right in the very center of the town, and all those who could, hastened to find points of vantage from which the impending battle could be viewed in safety. It took the City Marshal some little time to get his men together, as both Wyatt and Holliday were still sound asleep in bed, and getting word to them and the time it took for them to get up and dress themselves and get to the place where Verge and Morgan were in waiting, necessarily caused some little delay. The invaders, who had been momentarily expecting an attack, could not understand the cause of this delay, and finally concluded that the Earps were afraid and did not intend to attack them, at any rate while they were in the corral. This conclusion caused them to change their plan of battle. They instantly resolved that if ''The mountain

28

would not come to Mahomet—Mahomet would go to the mountain." If the Earps would not come to the corral, they would go and hunt up the Earps. Their horses were nearby, saddled, bitted and ready for instant use. Each man took his horse by the bridle-line and led him through the corral-gate to the street where they intended to mount.

But just as they reached the street, and before they had time to mount their horses, the Earp party came round the corner. Both sides were now within ten feet of each other. There were four men on a side, every one of whom had during his career been engaged in other shooting scrapes and were regarded as being the most desperate of desperate men. The horses gave the rustlers quite an advantage in the position. The Earps were in the open street, while the invaders used their horses for breast-works. Virgil Earp, as the City Marshal, ordered the Clantons and McLowrys to throw up their hands and surrender. This order they replied to with a volley from their pistols. The fight was now on. The Earps pressed in close, shooting as rapidly as they could. The fight was hardly started before it was over, and the result showed that nearly every shot fired by the Earp party went straight home to the mark.

Further Developments of the Feud

As soon as the smoke of battle cleared away sufficiently to permit of an accounting being made, it was seen that the two McLowrys and Billy Clanton were killed. They had been hit by no less than a half dozen bullets each and died in their tracks. Morgan Earp was the only one of the Marshal's force that

TOMBSTONE.

29

got hit. It was nothing more, however, than a slight flesh wound in one of his arms. Ike Clanton made his escape, but in doing so stamped himself as a coward of the first magnitude. No sooner had the shooting commenced than he threw down his pistol and with both hands high above his head, he ran to Wyatt Earp and begged him not to kill him. Here again Wyatt showed the kind of stuff that was in him, for instead of killing Clanton as most any other man would have done under the circumstances, he told him to run and get away, and he did.

The Earp party were all tried for the killing, and after a preliminary examination lasting several weeks, during which more than a hundred witnesses were examined, they were all exonerated. There were at this time two other outlaw bands in the country, who, when they heard of the killing of the McLowry brothers and Billy Clanton, swore to wipe out the Earp family and all their friends. They had no notion, however, of giving the Earps any more battles in the open. In the future, killings would be done from ambush, and the first one to get potted by this guerrilla system of warfare was Virge Earp, the City Marshal. As he was crossing one of the most prominent corners in Tombstone one night he was fired upon by some one not then known, but who was afterwards learned to be "Curly Bill," who was concealed behind the walls of a building that was then in course of construction on one of the corners. A shot-gun loaded with buck shot was the weapon used. Most of the charge struck Verge in the left arm between the shoulder and elbow, shattering the bone in a frightful manner. One or two other shot hit him but caused no serious injury. He was soon able to be about again, but never had any use afterwards of his left arm. As a matter of course the shock he sustained when the buck shot hit him caused him to fall, and the would-be assassin, thinking he had turned the trick successfully, made his escape in the dark to the foot-hills. The next to get murdered was Morgan Earp, who was shot through a window one night while playing a game of pin-pool with a friend.

Wyatt then realized that it was only a question of time until he and all of his friends would be killed in the same manner as his brother, if he remained in town. So he organized a party consisting of himself, "Doc" Holliday, Jack Vermillion, Sherman McMasters and Bill Johnson, and after equipping it with horses, guns and plenty of ammunition, started out on the war-path intending to hunt down and kill every one he could find who had had any hand in the murder of his brother Morgan and the attempted assassination of Verge. Wyatt had in the meantime learned that Pete Spence, Frank Stillwell, and a Mexican, by the name of Florentine, were the three who were interested in the killing of Morgan. Pete Spence had a ranch about twenty-five miles from Tombstone near the Dragoon Mountains, which was in reality nothing more than a rendezvous for cattle thieves and stage robbers.

Wyatt and his party headed straight for the Spence ranch as soon as he left Tombstone on his campaign of revenge. He found only the Mexican when he reached the ranch, and after making some inquiry as to the whereabouts of Spence, and learning that he had left early that morning for Tombstone by a different route from the one the Earps had traveled, proceeded, without further ceremony, to shoot the Mexican to pieces with buck shot. They left the greaser's body where it fell, and returned to Tombstone, where they expected to find Spence. He was there all right enough, but seeming to anticipate what Wyatt intended doing, had gone to the sheriff, who was not on friendly terms with the Earp faction, and surrendered, having himself locked up in jail.

Of course, Wyatt had to let him go for the time being, and was getting ready to start out on another expedition when he received word from Tucson that Frank Stillwell and Ike Clanton were there. Wyatt and "Doc" Holliday immediately started for Benson, where they took the train for Tucson which was about sixty miles farther south. Both were armed with shot guns, and just before the train came to a stop at the Tucson station, Wyatt and Holliday, from the platform of the rear coach saw Clanton and Stillwell standing on the depot platform. They immediately jumped off and started for the depot, intending to kill them both, but they were seen coming by the quarry who had evidently been made aware of Earp's movements and were on the lookout at the station. Clanton and Stillwell started to run as soon as they saw Wyatt and Holliday approaching, Stillwell down the railroad track and Clanton towards town. Wyatt and Holliday immediately gave chase to Stillwell and succeeded after a short run in overtaking him. He threw up his hands and begged not to be killed, but it was too late. Besides, Wyatt had given instructions that no prisoners should be taken, so they riddled his body with buck shot and left it lay where it fell, just as they had the Mexican. Wyatt and Holliday then returned to Tombstone, thinking there might still be a chance to get a crack at Pete Spence, but the latter still clung to the jail.

THE SHERIFF OF TOMBSTONE AND HIS CONSTITUENTS.

"Prairie Dog" Dave Morrow,
a Dodge Peace Officer

Ben Clark, a Famous Scout
and Indian Fighter

"Ed" Schieffelin.

Defying the Sheriff of Tombstone

Meanwhile the sheriff of Tombstone had received telegraphic instructions from the sheriff of Tucson to arrest Wyatt and Holliday as soon as they showed up, for the murder of Stillwell. When Wyatt got back to town he hustled his men together for the purpose of going out after Curly Bill, whom he believed to be the man who had shot Verge from ambush. When the sheriff and his posse reached Wyatt, the latter and his crowd were about to mount their horses preparatory to going on the "Curly Bill" expedition.

"Wyatt, I want to see you," said the sheriff.

"You will see me once too often," replied Wyatt as he bounded into the saddle. "And remember," continued Wyatt to the sheriff, "I am going to get that hound you are protecting in jail when I come back, if I have to tear the jail down to do it."

The sheriff made no further attempt to arrest Wyatt and Holliday. The next night Wyatt killed Curly Bill at the Whetstone Springs, about thirty miles from Tombstone, and just to make his word good with the sheriff, he and his party returned to town. The sheriff, however, had during his absence released Spence and told him to get across the Mexican border with as little delay as possible if he valued his life, for the Earp gang would surely kill him if he didn't.

This ended the Earp campaign in Arizona for the time being. Much has been written about Wyatt Earp that is the veriest rot, and every once in a while a newspaper article will appear in which it is alleged that some person had taken a fall out of him, and that when he had been put to the test, had shown the white feather. Not long ago a story was published in the different newspapers throughout the country that some little Canadian police officer somewhere in the Canadian Northwest had given Wyatt an awful call-down; had, in fact, taken his pistol from him and in other ways humiliated him. The story went like wild-fire, as all such stories do, and was printed and reprinted in all the big dailies in the country. There was not one word of truth in it, and the newspaper fakir who unloaded the story on the reading public very likely got no more than ten dollars for his work. Wyatt, to begin with, was never in the Canadian Northwest, and therefore was never in a position where a little Canadian police-officer could have taken such liberties with him as those described by the author of the story. Take it from me, no one has ever humiliated this man Earp, nor made him show the white feather under any circumstances whatever. While he is now a man past sixty, there are still a great many so-called bad men in this country who would be found, if put to the test, to be much easier game to tackle than this same lean and lanky Earp.

Wyatt Earp, like many more men of his character who lived in the West in its early days, has excited, by his display of great courage and nerve under trying conditions, the envy and hatred of those small-minded creatures with which the world seems to be abundantly peopled, and whose sole delight in life seems to be in fly-specking the reputations of real men. I have known him since the early seventies and have always found him a quiet, unassuming man, not given to brag or bluster, but at all times and under all circumstances a loyal friend and an equally dangerous enemy.

A PEACE CONVENTION AT FORT SCOTT, KANSAS

Famous Gun Fighters of the Western Frontier

Luke Short

by W. B. (Bat) Masterson

Luke Short
Twenty years ago he figured in as many affairs, where it was only the first shot that counted, as any man in the West.

THE subject of this narrative might have "died with his boots on," for he had many chances—but he didn't. The fact that he lived to die in bed, with his boots removed, as all good folk like to do when the end has come, may have been due to good luck, but I hardly think so. That he was the quickest at the critical moment is, perhaps, the best answer.

When the time came for Luke Short to pass out of this life—to render up the ghost as it were—he was able to lie down in bed in a home that was his own, surrounded by wife and friends, and peacefully await the coming of the end.

There was nothing in his wan and drawn features, as he lay on that last bed of sickness at Fort Worth, Texas, to indicate that luck had ever been his friend. He was aware that his time had come, and was reconciled to his fate. Every lineament in that cold, stern face, upon which death had already left its impress, showed defiance. He could almost be heard to say: "Death! You skulking coward! I know you are near; I also realize I cannot defeat you; but, if you will only make yourself visible for one brief moment, I will try!"

That he was willing to try, no matter how great the odds might be against him, was the one trait in his character that was ever conspicuously present.

Was Known as a "White Indian"

Luke was a little fellow, so to speak, about five feet, six inches in height, and weighing in the neighborhood of one hundred and forty pounds. It was a small package, but one of great dynamic force. In this connection it will not be out of order for me to state that, though of small build, it required a 7⅛ hat to fit his well-shaped, round head. At the time he left his father's ranch in western Texas, where he had been occupied as a cowboy in the middle seventies, for the Red Cloud Agency in North Dakota, he was nothing more than a white Indian. That is, he was an Indian in every respect except color. And, as nearly all of our American Indians living west of the Missouri River in those days were both wild and hostile and on the war path most of the time, a fair idea of Luke Short may be gleaned from this statement. Luke had received none of the advantages of a school in his younger days; he could hardly write his name legibly. It was, indeed, doubtful if he had ever seen a schoolhouse until he reached man's estate. But he could ride a broncho and throw a lariat; he could shoot both fast and straight, and was not afraid.

He had no sooner reached the northern boundary line of Nebraska, hard by the Sioux Indian Reservation, than he established what he was pleased to call a "trading ranch."

His purpose was to trade with the Sioux Indians, whose reservation was just across the line in North Dakota. Instinctively he knew that the Indians loved whiskey, and as even in those days he carried on his shoulders something of a commercial head, he conceived the idea that a gallon of whiskey worth ninety cents was not a bad thing to trade an Indian for a buffalo robe worth ten dollars. Accordingly Luke proceeded to lay in a goodly supply of "Pine Top," the name by which the whiskey traded to the Indians in exchange for their robes was known.

Uncle Sam Objects to His Business

He was not long in building up a lucrative business; nor was it long before the Indian chiefs of the Sioux tribe got on to him. Drunken bands of young bucks were regularly returning to their villages from the direction of the Short rendezvous, loaded to the muzzle with "Pine Top," and, as every drink contained at least two fights and as it usually took about ten drinks to cause an Indian to forget that the Great White Father abode in Washington, the condition of those who had found entertainment at the Short ranch, when they reached their camp, can better be imagined than told.

The Indian agent in charge of this particular branch of the Sioux tribe with whom Short had been dealing soon got busy with Washington. He represented to the Department of the Interior that a band of cutthroat white men, under the leadership of Luke Short, were trading whiskey to his Indians, and that he was powerless to stop it, as the camp of the white men was located just across the reservation line, in the State of Nebraska, which was outside of his jurisdiction. He requested the government to instantly remove the whiskey traders and drive them from the country. Otherwise, said he, and Indian uprising will surely follow. The government, as was to be expected, forthwith instructed the post commander at Omaha to get after the purveyors of the poisonous "Pine Top," who were charged with causing such havoc among the noble red men of the Sioux reservation.

36

The military commander at Omaha soon had a company of United States cavalry after Short, and, as he had no notice of such a move being made against him, he was soon a prisoner in the hands of the government authorities. He was alone in his little dugout, cooking his dinner, when the soldiers arrived. He was told that he was a prisoner, by order of the government, for having unlawfully traded whiskey to the Indians.

"Is that all, gentlemen?" said Luke, as he invited the officer in command of the soldiers to sit down and have a bite to eat with him.

"There will be no time for eating," said the officer, "as we must reach Sidney by tomorrow morning, in time to catch the Overland train for Omaha. So get together what things you care to take along, and we will be on our way."

"I have nothing that I care to take along," Luke replied, "excepting what I have on;" and as that mostly consisted of a pair of Colt's pistols and a belt of cartridges, the officer soon had them in his custody.

"Where are your partners?" queried the Captain.

"I have no partners," replied Short. "I've been running this ranch by myself."

But Luke did have a partner, who was at that very time in Sidney procuring provisions and more "Pine Top."

After everything around the ranch resembling whiskey had been destroyed by order of the officer in command, the trip to Sidney, about seventy-five miles away, was taken up. Luke was put astride a government horse, his feet fastened with a rope underneath the animal's girth, and told to ride in the center of the company of cavalrymen. Sidney was reached in time to catch the Overland train, and Luke was hustled aboard with as little ceremony as possible.

Luke had, by his quiet and diffident manner during the short time he had been prisoner, succeeded in having the officer regard him in the light of a harmless little adventurer, who really did not seem capable, even if so disposed, of committing a crime of any sort; and for this reason did not have him either handcuffed or shackled, after placing him aboard the train for Omaha.

Sidney, Nebraska, was a very small place in those days. The permanent population in all probability did not exceed the thousand mark. Sidney, following the custom of all small hamlets, however, would turn out when there was anything unusual going on. And the sight of a company of United States soldiers lined up at the railroad station was enough to arouse her curiosity and cause her townsfolk to turn out in a body and investigate the cause. Luke Short's partner was among those who came to see the big show at the depot, and his surprise can well be imagined when he discovered that no less a person than his partner was responsible for the big event. It did not take Luke and his partner long to fix up a code of signals by which they could communicate with each other. Luke could say a few things in the Indian langauge that his partner could understand, and to which he could make comprehensible reply.

CHESTNUT STREET, LEADVILLE.

38

Short Escapes from the Soldiers

"Skidoo" and "Twenty-three" were terms familiar to Short, even in those days. But they were conveyed by the sign language instead of being spoken as now.

Luke made his partner understand that he would soon be back in Sidney, and to have everything in readiness, so that they could skip the country with as little delay as possible, as soon as he showed up. The charge of having unlawfully traded whiskey to the Indians did not seem to concern him in the least. "I can beat that sure," he said to himself; "but supposing that agent should take a notion to call for a count of heads. What then? I know that there are several young bucks, whom I caught trying to steal my 'Pine Top,' who will not be there to answer roll-call, in case one is ordered. I planted those bucks myself and, outside of my partner, no one knows the exact location of the cache. While I have no notion of putting in a claim against the government for the work, I must be careful and avoid having it endeavor to show that I really did perform such service."

These were perhaps the thoughts he was conveying by signals to his partner when he boarded the train at Sidney that was to take him to Omaha.

To state the story briefly. Luke did not tarry long with the soldiers after the train left Sidney. That night found Luke back in town, and before the following morning both he and his partner were well on their way to Colorado, driving a big span of mules hitched to a canvas-covered wagon.

This happened in the fall of 1878 and, as Leadville was just then having a big mining boom, Luke headed for Denver.

It must be remembered that in that country in those days there were no settlements of any kind and, by keeping from the line of the railroad, a white person was seldom seen.

A Little Affair in Leadville

Luke and his partner arrived in Denver in due course of time, and drove to one of the city horse corrals, where next day they disposed of their outfit at a good price. Luke's partner returned to his home in Austin, Texas, where his family connections were both wealthy and prominent. Luke went to Leadville, where everything was then on the boom. Here he began to associate with a class of people far different in manner, taste and dress from those he had been accustomed to. He was thrown in the society of rich mine buyers, as well as mining promoters. He got acquainted with gamblers and the keepers of the mining camp "honkatonks."

The whole thing was a new life to him, and he took to it like a duck to water. It was the first place where he saw the game of faro dealt, and he was fascinated. He was not long in camp before he was talked about. He ran foul of a bad man with a gun one day in one of the camp's prominent gambling houses, and the bad man, who had a record of having killed someone somewhere, attempted to take some sort of liberty with one of Luke's bets and, when the latter politely requested the bad man to keep his hands off, the bad man became very angry and made some rude remarks. The dealer was frightened half out of his wits. He looked to see Short shot full of holes before anyone could raise a hand to prevent it. The dealer, of course, didn't have Luke's number. He knew the other fellow, but had yet to become acquainted with the late vendor of "Pine Top" up Nebraska way.

"Gentlemen," said the dealer, in his most suave manner, "I will make the amount of the bet good, rather than have a quarrel."

"You will not make anything good to me," said Short. "That is my bet, and I will not permit anyone to take it."

"You insignificant little shrimp," growled the bad man, at the same time reaching for his cannister. "I will shoot your hand off, if you dare to put it on that bet."

But he didn't. Nor did he get his pistol out of his hip pocket. For, quicker than a flash, Luke had jammed his own pistol into the bad man's face and pulled the trigger, and the bad man rolled over on the floor. The bullet passed through his cheek but, luckily, did not kill him.

There was no arrest or trial. Such things were happening all the time in those days in Leadville. This, however, gave Luke quite a standing. He was soon in big demand. Gambling-house proprietors wanted him to stay around their places of business during the busy hours, so as to keep the bad men in camp from carrying off their bank rolls. He had a faculty of making friends, and was soon popular with the quieter and better class of the sporting fraternity. He learned to play cards, and was soon dealing faro. No one who saw him then, togged out in tailor-made clothes and a derby hat, would have recognized in him the man who took the header from the Overland train ten miles east of Sidney, when he made the get-away from the soldiers.

Snuffing out a Gambler

The spring of 1881 found Luke Short in Tombstone, Arizona, dealing faro in a house managed by Wyatt Earp.

One morning I went into the Oriental gambling house, where Luke was working, just in time to keep him from killing a gambler named Charlie Storms. There was scarcely any difference between this case and the one with the bad man in Leadville a couple of years previous. Charlie Storms was one of the best-known gamblers in the entire West and had, on several occasions, successfully defended himself in pistol fights with Western "gun-fighters."

Charlie Storms and I were very close friends,—as much so as Short and I were—and for that reason I did not care to see him get into what I knew would be a very serious difficulty. Storms did not know Short and, like the bad man in Leadville, had sized him up as an insignificant-looking fellow, whom he could slap in the face without expecting a return. Both men were about to pull their pistols when I jumped between them and grabbed Storms, at the same time requesting Luke not to shoot,—a request I knew he would respect if it was possible without endangering his own life too much. I had no trouble in getting Storms out of the house, as he knew me to be his friend. When Storms and I reached the street I advised him to go to his room and take a sleep, for I then learned for the first time that he had been up all night, and had been quarreling with other persons.

He asked me to accompany him to his room, which I did, and after seeing him safely in his apartments, where I supposed he could go to bed, I returned to where Short was. I was just explaining to Luke that Storms was a very decent sort of man when, lo and behold! there he stood before us. Without saying a word, he took hold of Luke's arm and pulled him off the sidewalk, where he had been standing, at the same time pulling his pistol, a Colt's cut-off, 45 calibre, single action; but like the Leadvillian, he was too slow, although he succeeded in getting his pistol out. Luke stuck the muzzle of his own pistol against Storms' heart and pulled the trigger. The bullet tore the heart asunder, and as he was falling, Luke shot him again. Storms was dead when he hit the ground. Luke was given a preliminary hearing before a magistrate and exonerated.

The Story of Two Rival Shows

In the spring of 1883 Luke formed a partnership with Harris and Beeson of Dodge City, and operated the Long Branch saloon, the biggest and best-paying gambling house in Dodge at the time. The mayor of Dodge, whose name was Webster, was also running a gambling house and saloon next door to that operated by Short. At this time Dodge City was the shipping point for the Texas cattle driven every summer from the great cattle ranges of western Texas to the northern markets.

A fortune was to be made every season by the gambling house that could control this trade and, as Short was from Texas and had once been a cowboy himself, he held the whip-hand over the mayor, so far, at any rate, as the patronage of the cattlemen was concerned. This the mayor did not relish and, as he was a stubborn and strong-minded man himself, who would brook no opposition if he could help it, he set to work to put Luke out of the business. He had an ordinance passed by the City Council, prohibiting music in all the gambling houses and saloons in the city. Short employed a band in his place of business and Webster did likewise; but the latter was the mayor and therefore in control of the situation, so he thought. The city marshal was instructed by the mayor to notify Short that the music in his place must be discontinued.

"That suits me," Luke is reported to have told the marshal. "I don't need music in my house in order to do business and, besides, maintaining a band is quite an item of expense."

The following night the only house in the city in which there was music was that operated by the mayor. Luke then smelt a mouse.

"We'll see about this," remarked Luke to his partners, Beeson and Harris.

The next night he re-engaged the band and instructed it to go ahead grinding out the old familiar melodies, so dear to the heart of the Texas cowboy. Luke remained about the place for several hours to see what move, if any, was to be made by the mayor. As he saw nothing to cause alarm, he concluded to go away for a while and pay a visit to a sick friend. He had not left the place more than ten minutes before all the members of the band, among them one woman, the pianist, were arrested and locked up in the city calaboose.

Forced to Leave the Town

Luke was notified, and came hurriedly down to the saloon. He learned the facts of the arrest and went out to hunt up the officer who was in charge of the squad in order that he might furnish bail for the musicians and have them released. But he could not find him or any other person who was considered competent to accept a bail bond. All the time Luke was trying to get his employees out of the calaboose, the music in the mayor's place was in full swing. This, as can well be imagined, did not tend to help matters in the least. About the time Luke had made up his mind that nothing could be done that night towards the reease of the prisoners, he saw the officer whom he had been looking for standing some little distance away. Luke started towards him.

The officer, who was standing on the sidewalk, which was a foot or so above the street, saw Luke coming, and instantly pulled his pistol and fired point blank at him. The shot missed and Luke returned the fire; but just as he pulled the trigger the officer started to run, and in leaving the sidewalk for the dark street he fell. Luke, thinking he had hit him, went then to his place of business, secured a shot gun and stood off the town until morning. He accomplished this by refusing to submit to arrest that night.

The next morning he was prevailed upon to lay aside his weapons, go over to the police court, plead guilty to creating a disturbance, pay a fine and have the whole thing ended. That was what had been promised him if he would take off his arms and surrender to the officers. He accordingly gave up his pistols and started for the police court with the officers. But instead of them taking him to the police court, as they promised, they took him to the city jail and kept him locked up until the noon trains arrived. The passenger trains going East and West passed each other at Dodge, and Luke was marched to the depot by an escort armed with shotguns and told to choose which train he would take. There was nothing left for him to do. They had him, and were only waiting an excuse to riddle him with buckshot if he offered the least resistance.

He took the East-bound train and landed in Kansas City.

Lining Up for a Big Fight

I was in Denver at the time, and he wired me to come to Kansas City at once, which I did. We talked the matter over when we met, and concluded to up to Topeka and place the matter before the Governor. The next day we did so. The Governor denounced the conduct of the Dodge City authorities, but said that he could do nothing, as the local authorities at Dodge had informed him that they were amply able to preserve the peace and did not desire state interference. We stated to the Governor that we believed we were able to rehabilitate ourselves in Dodge, but did not care to run afoul state authorities, in case we concluded to do so. The Governor told us to go ahead and re-establish ourselves, if we could; that he would keep off, and wished us luck. Immediately I started for Silverton, Colorado, where Wyatt Earp was located at the time, and enlisted him in our cause. Luke went to Caldwell, Kansas, where he had a couple of staunch friends, who were willing to take the bit in their mouths and go to the front and fight his battles whenever called upon.

42

Inside of a week from the time Luke and I separated in Kansas City, we had our forces organized and were on the way to Dodge. It was decided that if a fight was all that would satisfy the mayor of Dodge,—a fight he would have.

Wyatt was selected to land in Dodge first. With him, but unknown to the Dodge authorities, were several desperate men. Several more dropped into town unobserved by the enemy. It finally became whispered about that Wyatt Earp had a strong force of desperate men already domiciled in town in the interest of Luke Short. The mayor called a hasty meeting of his friends, and after they had all assembled in the council chamber of the city hall, informed them solemnly of what he had heard about the Earp invasion. Anyone who was present at that meeting could easily have seen that anything but a fight was what the mayor and his friends were looking for, now that such a thing was not altogether improbable. Someone present suggested that Wyatt be invited to attend the meeting and state, if he would, his position in the matter. The suggestion met with the instant approval of all present, and the mayor proceeded to forthwith appoint a committee to call upon Earp and inform him of its action. Wyatt was soon found, and told of the wishes of the assembled patriots.

A Conference with the Enemy

"It will afford me great pleasure to attend your meeting," was the laconic reply of the noble Warwick, and he was soon the central figure of as fine a collection of cutthroats as ever scuttled ship.

The mayor, addressing Wyatt, made inquiry as to the truth of the report that he and numerous other desperate men were in the city for the purpose of reinstating Short in Dodge.

"Mr. Mayor, and gentlemen of the meeting," said Wyatt; "I guess the report is true. I came here some days ago," said he; "and, thinking that perhaps something might happen where I would need assistance, brought along some other gentlemen who signified a willingness to join in whatever festivities might arise."

"Moreover," continued Wyatt, "Luke and Bat will each arrive at noon tomorrow, and on their arrival we expect to open up hostilities."

"Now, look here, Wyatt," said the mayor, "you have no better friends anywhere than we are, and we don't want any more fighting in this town. There has already been enough shooting and killing in Dodge to do for a while. Now, why can't this thing be fixed up before it goes any farther?"

"It can," said Wyatt, "if you are willing to allow Luke to return and conduct his business unmolested as heretofore."

"I am perfectly willing to agree to that," said Webster. "And so are we," sung out the meeting in a chorus.

"All right, gentlemen," replied the phlegmatic Mr. Earp, "there shall be no conflict. I will proceed to inform both Mr. Short and Mr. Masterson of your decision in the case, and I will guarantee that if you keep your part of the agreement there shall be no bloodshed."

Wyatt immediately notified Short and I by wire of the complete backdown of the enemy, and when we reached the city next day we were cordially received by our friends. The enemy, not being sure that Wyatt could control the situation, kept in the background until he had received assurances from both Short and I that the peace terms made by Earp would be faithfully lived up to by us.

As soon as things quieted down a little, Short sent for the mayor and sheriff to meet him and some of his friends at his place of business for the purpose of talking over the situation and arriving at a better understanding. The mayor and sheriff came and with them the city attorney and the prosecuting attorney of the county. Short's party consisted of himself, his two partners, Beeson and Harris, Wyatt Earp and myself.

Humiliating His Honor the Mayor

Luke addressed the mayor something after this fashion, after we had all settled down in our chairs:

"Mr. Webster, you have on the police force of this city two men who, without any reason known to me, showed themselves during the late trouble to be bitter enemies of mine. I want them removed from the force."

The mayor assured Luke that he need not give himself any further concern on that score, as both men complained of had already handed in their resignations and left town.

"Very well," said Luke. "There is, however, another thing I wish to call to your notice. You had an ordinance passed by the city council prohibiting music in saloons. I want that ordinance repealed."

"It shall be done," said the mayor, and turning to the city attorney, instructed him to prepare a call for a special meeting of the council and to draw up an ordinance calling for the repeal of the objectionable one.

This ended Short's business with the mayor. He then turned to the sheriff and said in substance:

"Mr. Sheriff, you also have two men in your office that are objectionable to me and I would like to have you remove them." He then named the men, and the sheriff promised that they would have to go.

"Here are the names of the men you can appoint in their place," and he handed the sheriff a piece of paper containing the names of the men he desired appointed.

"All right, Luke," said the sheriff, "they are good enough for me."

Luke then turned around to the prosecuting attorney of the county and said, "I furnished bail for Mr. Blank in the sum of $2,000 before I was ordered to leave town, and I want that bail bond containing my name returned to me and all record of it destroyed."

"That will be easy," said the prosecutor.

"Now, gentlemen," said Luke, "there being nothing further to do, suppose we return to the bar and take a little something just for old times' sake."

"All right," said everybody present, and the procession to the bar started.

Luke had won a bloodless battle, but that such was the case was no fault of his, for he had been willing to fight at any and all stages of the proceedings.

Short Owns the Town Again

We subsequently found that when Mayor Webster learned how he had been trapped by Earp, he hunted up the sheriff and prosecuting attorney and sent a hurry-up telegram to the Governor, which was signed by all three of them, requesting him to send with as little delay as possible two companies of militia, assuring him that unless that was immediately done, a great tragedy would surely be enacted in the streets of Dodge City. The Governor, anticipating just such a move as this on the part of the authorities at Dodge as soon as they got frightened—and the telegram calling for militia strongly indicated that that time had now arrived,—refused point blank to send the militia, and reminded the senders of the message that they had already repeatedly assured him that they were sufficiently able to handle the situation and did not need the militia; "and," said the Governor, in concluding his reply, "I expect you to do it."

When it became known in Dodge the sort of a reply the Governor had sent back to the appeal for militia, something of consternation took possession of the mayor's followers. Those who had lately been the loudest in their declarations of hostility to Short were now for peace at any price.

Webster, himself no coward, saw that the yellow streak he knew was in the makeup of his followers was giving unmistakable signs of recrudescence. He knew that when the time came he would have to fight the battle alone. He remembered that those very men upon whom he would now have to rely for support had already hid themselves from Short the night of the arrest of the musicians, and he could well imagine what they were likely to do now that Short had been strongly reinforced. It was at this stage of affairs that Webster concluded to send for Wyatt, and if possible bring about a settlement of the difficulty without an appeal to arms. In making this move the mayor acted both wisely and timely; for had the case gone over to the next day there would have, in all probability, been bloodshed on both sides.

Luke, soon after his restoration to Dodge, concluded to settle up his affairs and move to Texas. He somehow could not bring himself to like those with whom he had so recently been on the outs, and that fall sold out all his interests in Kansas to his partners, and went to Texas.

The fall of 1884 found him the proprietor of the White Elephant gambling house in Fort Worth. The White Elephant was one of the largest and costliest establishments of its kind in the entire Southwest at the time. As a matter of course he made plenty of money, but it required a lot of money to keep him going, for he was one of the best-hearted men who ever lived. He could not say no to anyone, and, as might be expected, was continually being imposed upon by professional "cadgers," who make it a point to borrow all they can and never pay back anything. While he made fortunes in his gambling establishments, he died a comparatively poor man. He perhaps owed less and had more money due him when he died than any gambler who ever lived.

In the spring of 1887 I visited Short in Fort Worth, and learned soon after my arrival that he was having some trouble which was likely to end seriously with a notorious local character by the name of Jim Courtright. It appears that this fellow Courtright, who had killed a couple of men in Fort Worth, also a couple more in New Mexico, and was therefore dreaded by almost the entire community, asked Short to install him as a special officer in the White Elephant. Luke, who had been a substantial friend of Courtright's during his trouble at Fort Worth, told him he could not think of such a thing.

"Why, Jim," said Luke, " I would rather pay you a good salary to stay away from my house entirely."

"You know," continued Luke, "that the people about here are all afraid of you, and your presence in my house as an officer would ruin my business."

Courtright, who was a sullen, ignorant bully, with no sense of right or wrong, could not see it as Luke did. He could not understand that it was a pure matter of business and would be much better for Short to hire him to stay away from the house altogether than to have him coming around it. At any rate, Courtright got huffy at Luke and threatened to have him indicted and his place closed up. Courtright could not get it through his head how it was that Luke had dared to turn him down. He knew that he had everybody else in town "buffaloed" and could see no reason why Luke should be different from the others.

Luke and I were sitting together in the billiard room of the "White Elephant" one evening, discussing the trouble he was having with Courtright and the effect it was likely to have on his business.

Just then one of Luke's business associates, by the name of Jake Johnson, came to where we were sitting and informed Luke that Courtright was in the outer lobby and would like to have a talk with him.

"Tell him to come in," said Short.

"I did invite him in," replied Johnson, "but he refused and said I was to tell you to come out."

"Very well," said Luke, "I will see what he has to say; and immediately got up and accompanied Johnson to where Courtright was in waiting.

It did not take Luke very long after meeting Courtright to discover that the latter's mission was anything but one of peace. He brought along no olive branch, but instead a brace of pistols, conspicuously displayed. It was not a parley that he came for, but fight, and his demeanor indicated a desire that hostilities open up forthwith.

No time was wasted in the exchange of words once the men faced each other. Both drew their pistols at the same time, but, as usual, Short's spoke first and a bullet from a Colt's 45-calibre pistol went crashing through Courtright's body. The shock caused him to reel backward; then he got another and still another, and by the time his lifeless form had reached the floor, Luke had succeeded in shooting him five times.

Luke was arrested on the spot by a deputy sheriff, and taken to the county jail, where he remained during the night. The next day he was taken before a justice of the peace, who held him for the grand jury in a nominal bond. This ended the case, as the grand jury refused to indict on the evidence, holding that it was a case of justifiable homicide.

This ended Luke Short's shooting scrapes with the exception of a little gun dispute three years later at Fort Worth which had no fatal results.

I took occasion at the opening of this story to state that when Luke reached the age of young manhood he was totally lacking in education. It is now but proper for me to say that at the time of his death, twenty years later, he was an exceptionally well-read man. He could write an excellent letter; always used good English when talking and could quote Shakespeare, Byron, Goldsmith and Longfellow better and more accurately than most scholars.

To the burning of the midnight oil was due the transformation. It transformed him from a white Indian, when I first found him, to a diffident, courteous gentleman, who was, at his death about twelve years ago, one of the best known and most popular sporting men in this country.

Jim Courtright, Once Marshal of Ft. Worth

ROBBERY OF THE MONTANA COACH.

Famous Gun Fighters of the Western Frontier

"Doc" Holliday

bt W. B. (Bat) Masterson

John H. (Doc) Holliday
A well-known gambler and gun-fighter who had a stormy career in the West during the late seventies

WHILE he never did anything to entitle him to a statue in the Hall of Fame, Doc Holliday was nevertheless a most picturesque character on the western border in those days when the pistol instead of law courts determined issues. Holliday was a product of the state of Georgia, and a scion of a most respectable and prominent family. He graduated as a dentist from one of the medical colleges of his native state before he left it, but did not follow his profession very long after receiving his diploma. It was perhaps too respectable a calling for him.

Holliday had a mean disposition and an ungovernable temper, and under the influence of liquor was a most dangerous man. In this respect he was very much like the big Missourian who had put in the day at a cross-road groggery and, after getting pretty well filled up with bug juice of the Moonshine brand, concluded that it was about time for him to say something that would make an impression on his hearers; so he straightened up, threw out his chest and declared in a loud tone of voice, that he was "a bad man when he was drinking, and managed to keep pretty full all the time." So it was with Holliday.

Couldn't Have Whipped a Boy

Physically, Doc Holliday was a weakling who could not have whipped a healthy fifteen-year old boy in a go-as-you-please fist fight, and no one knew this better than himself, and the knowledge of this fact was perhaps why he was so ready to resort to a weapon of some kind whenever he got himself into

49

difficulty. He was hot-headed and impetuous and very much given to both drinking and quarrelling, and, among men who did not fear him, was very much disliked.

He possessed none of the qualities of leadership such as those that distinguished such men as H. P. Myton, Wyatt Earp, Billy Tilghman and other famous western characters. Holliday seemed to be absolutely unable to keep out of trouble for any great length of time. He would no sooner be out of one scrape before he was in another, and the strange part of it is he was more often in the right than in the wrong, which has rarely ever been the case with a man who is continually getting himself into trouble.

The indiscriminate killing of some negroes in the little Georgia village in which he lived was what first caused him to leave his home. The trouble came about in rather an unexpected manner one Sunday afternoon—unexpected so far at least as the negroes were concerned. Near the little town in which Holliday was raised, there flowed a small river in which the white boys of the village, as well as the black ones, used to go in swimming together. The white boys finally decided that the negroes would have to find a swimming place elsewhere, and notified them to that effect. The negro boys were informed that in the future they would have to go further down the stream to do their swimming, which they promptly refused to do and told the whites that if they didn't like existing conditions, that they themselves would have to hunt up a new swimming hole.

Shot a Crowd of Negroes

As might have been expected in those days in the South, the defiant attitude taken by the negroes in the matter caused the white boys to instantly go upon the war path. They would have their order obeyed or know the reason why. One beautiful Sunday afternoon, while an unusually large number of negroes were in swimming at the point in dispute, Holliday appeared on the river bank with a double-barrelled shot-gun in his hands, and, pointing it in the direction of the swimmers, ordered them from the river.

"Get out, and be quick about it," was his peremptory command. The negroes, as a matter of course, stampeded for the opposite shore, falling over each other in their efforts to get beyond the range of the shot gun. Holliday waited until he got a bunch of them together, and then turned loose with both barrels, killing two outright, and wounding several others.

The shooting, as a matter of course, was entirely unjustifiable, as the negroes were on the run when killed; but the authorities evidently thought otherwise, for nothing was ever done about the matter. Holliday, afterwards in speaking about the occurrence, justified the deed on the broad grounds that the "niggers" had to be disciplined, and he knew of no more effective way of doing it than with a shot-gun. His family, however, thought it would be best for him to go away for a while and allow the thing to die out; so he accordingly pulled up stakes and went to Dallas, Texas, where he hung out his professional sign bearing the inscription, "J. H. Holliday, Dentist." This was in the early seventies and at the time when Dallas was a typical frontier town in everything the term implied. A stranger in Dallas in those days could get anything he

DENVER.

wanted from pitch and toss to man-slaughter at any hour of the day or night, and that was exactly what suited the Georgia dentist.

Gambling was not only the principal and best-paying industry of the town at the time, but it was also reckoned among its most respectable and, as the hectic Georgian had always shown a fondness for all things in which the elements of chance played an important part, his new environment furnished him with no cause for complaint. In a short time those who wished to consult professionally with the doctor, had to do so over a card table in some nearby gambling establishment, or not at all. While Holliday never boasted about the killing of the negroes down in Georgia, he was nevertheless regarded by his new-made Texas acquaintances who knew about the occurrence, as a man with a record; and a man with a record of having killed someone in those days, even though the victim was only a "nigger," was looked upon as something more than the ordinary mortal; wherefore the doctor on that account was given instant recognition by the higher circles of society in Dallas.

A Poker Game Incident

If there was any one thing above another Holliday loved better than a session in a poker game, it was conflict, and, as Dallas was the home of conflict, the doctor was in his element. It was not a "nigger" that he shot this time, but a white man of some local prominence for which he had to emigrate to some more congenial place. He brought up next at Jacksborro, a small, out-of-the way place just off the Fort Richardson Military Reservation, on the north-western border of the state, where civilization was only in a formative stage.

The doctor had by this time heard much about the man-killers who abode on the frontier, and regarded himself as well qualified to play a hand among the foremost of the guild. He was not long in Jacksborro before he was in another scrape. This time it was with a soldier who was stationed at the Fort, and who had been given permission to visit the town by his commanding officer. The trouble was over a card game in which the soldier claimed he had been given the worst of it by the man from Georgia. This of course, necessitated the fighting Georgian taking another trip on the road, for he knew it would never do to let the soldiers at the Fort capture him, which they would be sure to try to do as soon as word reached them about the killing of their comrade. He therefore lost no time in getting out of town, and, seated on the hurricane deck of a Texas cayuse, was well on his way to safety by the time the news of the homicide reached the Fort. It was a long and dangerous trip that he mapped out for himself on this occasion.

His Career in Denver

From Jacksborro to Denver, Colorado, was fully eight hundred miles, and, as much of the route to be traversed through was the Texas Panhandle and No-man's land, which was in those days alive with Indians none too friendly to the white man, and renegade Mexicans from New Mexico, the journey was a most perilous one to take; but the doughty doctor was equal to the task and in due time reached Denver without either having lost his scalp, or his desire for more conflict. This was in the summer of 1876 and while Denver was a much more important city than Dallas, its local government was conducted on very much the same principles. Like Dallas, everything went in Denver, and the doctor, after looking the situation over for a day or two, concluded that he had lost nothing by the change.

In all respects the Rocky Mountain town looked good to him, and as he had set out to build up a record for himself as a man-killer, he did not purpose lying idle very long. While Denver, in many respects in those days was a rough and ready town, it nevertheless enforced to the very letter the ordinance against the carrying of fire arms, and Holliday, for the nonce becoming prudent, put his cannister aside, but straightway went and bought himself a murderous looking knife. Thus heeled, he did not long delay in getting into action, and in so doing, carved up the face and neck of one Bud Ryan, a quiet and gentlemanly looking sport, in a frightful manner. Bud Ryan still lives in Denver, and carries around with him the marks of his run-in with the fighting Holliday, more than thirty years ago. It was again the doctor's turn to take the road and escape from the scene of his recent malefaction, and this time he headed for Dodge City, Kansas. It was there I first met him, although I had heard about his doings in Texas.

He was slim of build and sallow of complexion, standing about five feet ten inches, and weighing no more than 130 pounds. His eyes were of a pale blue and his moustache was thin and of a sandy hue. Dodge City was then very much like Dallas and Denver, only a little more so, and the doctor did not express regret at having come. It was easily seen that he was not a healthy man for he not only looked the part, but he incessantly coughed it as well. During his year's stay at Dodge at that time, he did not have a quarrel with anyone, and, although regarded as a sort of grouch, he was not disliked by those with whom he had become acquainted. It was during this time that he also made the acquaintance of Wyatt Earp and they were always fast friends ever afterwards.

His Friendship with Wyatt Earp

He went from Dodge to Trinidad, Colorado, where, within a week from the time he landed, he shot and seriously wounded a young sport by the name of Kid Colton, over a very trivial matter. He was again forced to hunt the tall timber and managed to make his escape to Las Vegas, New Mexico, which was then something of a boom town, on account of the Santa Fe Railroad having just reached there. Holliday remained around Las Vegas for some time, doing the best he could in a gambling way; then he had a quarrel with one of the town rounders by the name of Mike Gordon, whom he invited to step outside of the saloon in which they were quarrelling. No sooner had Gordon stepped from the door than Holliday shot him dead. From Las Vegas to Dodge City across country, without following the traveled road, was about five hundred miles and this was the trip Holliday was again compelled to make on horseback, in order to get away from the authorities who were hot on his trail. He reached Dodge City in safety and remained there until Wyatt Earp took him in his covered wagon to Arizona in the fall of 1880. Again he showed no disposition to quarrel or shoot while he lived in Dodge, and many thought that much of the trouble he had been having in other places had been forced upon him, but I am satisfied that it was pretty much all of his own seeking. His

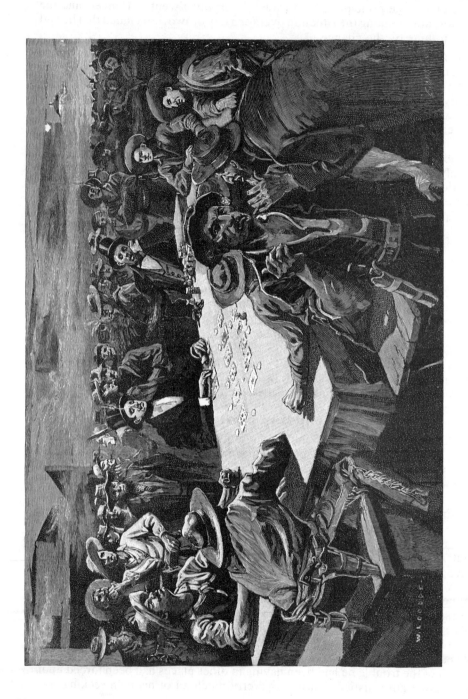

THE FARO PLAYERS.

whole heart and soul were wrapped up in Wyatt Earp and he was always ready to stake his life in defence of any cause in which Wyatt was interested. He aided the Earp brothers in their street fight in Tombstone, against the Clanton and McLowrie brothers, in which the latter two were killed, along with Billy Clanton.

It was Doc Holliday, who, along with Wyatt Earp, overtook and killed Frank Stillwell at the railroad station in Tucson for having participated in the murder of Morgan Earp in Tombstone. He was by Wyatt's side when he killed Curly Bill at the Whetstone Springs outside of Tombstone. Damon did no more for Pythias than Holliday did for Wyatt Earp.

After Wyatt and his party had run down and killed nearly all their enemies in Arizona, Holliday returned to Denver, where he was arrested on an order from the Arizona authorities, charged with aiding in the killing of Frank Stillwell. This happened in the spring of 1882. I was in Denver at the time, and managed to secure an audience with Governor Pitkin who, after listening to my statement in the matter, refused to honor the Arizona requisition for Holliday. I then had a complaint sworn out against Holliday, charging him with having committed a highway robbery in Pueblo, Colorado, and had him taken from Denver to Pueblo, where he was put under a nominal bond and released from custody. The charge of highway robbery made against Holliday, at this time, was nothing more than a subterfuge on my part to prevent him from being taken out of the state by the Arizona authorities, after Governor Pitkin went out of office, but the Colorado authorities did not know it at the time. Holliday always managed to have his case put off whenever it would come up for trial, and, by furnishing a new bond, in every instance would be released again.

When he died at Glenwood Springs a few years afterwards, he was still under bond to answer to the charge of highway robbery I had caused a certain person to prefer against him. Doc Holliday, whose right name was John H. Holliday, lived during his stormy career in three states of the Union besides the one in which he was born, and in two territories; namely Texas, Colorado, and Kansas, and in the territories of New Mexico and Arizona. Besides the killing of the negroes in the river in his home town, he shot a man in Dallas, Texas, and killed another in Jacksborro. He stabbed Bud Ryan in a frightful manner in Denver, Colorado, and shot another in Trinidad in the same state. He killed a man in Las Vegas, New Mexico, and was directly connected with several killings in Arizona.

Kansas, it will be observed, was the only state in which he had lived in which he failed to either slay or bodily wound some person. The question as to the extent in which he was justified in doing as he did, is of course open to debate. I have always believed that much of Holliday's trouble was caused by drink and for that reason held him to blame in many instances. While I assisted him substantially on several occasions, it was not because I liked him any too well, but on account of my friendship for Wyatt Earp who did.

Holliday had few real friends anywhere in the West. He was selfish and had a perverse nature—traits not calculated to make a man popular in the early days on the frontier.

GREGORY GOLD DIGGINGS, COLORADO, MAY, 1859.

Famous
Gun Fighters of
the Western Frontier

"Billy" Tilghman

by W. B. (Bat) Masterson

Bill Tilghman, a Graduate of the Buffalo Range, and U.S. Marshal of Oklahoma

NOTWITHSTANDING the discovery of gold in California in 1849, and at Pike's Peak, Colorado, ten years later, the civilizing of the West did not really commence until after the close of the Civil War. It was during the decade immediately following the ending of the conflict between the North and South that civilization west of the Missouri River first began to assume substantial form.

It was during this period that three great transcontinental lines of railroads were built, all of them starting at some point on the West Bank of the Missouri River. The Union Pacific from Omaha to Ogden, Utah, was completed during these years, also the Kansas Pacific, from Kansas City to Denver, Colorado, and the Atchison, Topeka and Santa Fe from Atchinson, Kansas, to Pueblo, Colorado.

In twenty years from the day the first railroad tie was laid on the roadbed of the Union Pacific at Omaha, our Western frontier had almost entirely disappeared. There has been no frontier in this country for a good many years. The railroads long ago did away with all there ever was of it. Railroad trains, with their Pullman car and dining-car connections, have been reaching almost every point in the West of any consequence for the last twenty years.

On what was once known as our great American plains, which, a generation ago, furnished a habitat for the wild Indian, the buffalo, the deer and the antelope, today can be seen thousands of beautiful homes, in which none of the evidences of higher civilization are lacking. While it required but twenty years or so to bring about this wonderful change in this vast territory, the task was by no means an easy one.

Let the reader remember that in those twenty years, no less than half a dozen bloody Indian wars were fought, and that the scenes of those conflicts extended from the Dakotas on the north to the lava beds of Oregon on the west, and south to the frontier of Texas; and a fairly good idea of the magnitude of the undertaking will be gained. It was during those stirring times that nearly all of the famous characters of our once immense frontier, many of whom are now but memories, played a conspicuous part in this vast theatre of human strife.

James B. Hickok (Wild Bill) was perhaps the only one of that chivalrous band of fighting men, who composed the vanguard of western civilization, who had acquired fame before the period I have named. When this most remarkable man came to the West at the close of the Civil War, in which he had taken a conspicuous part both in south-west Missouri and in the campaign along the Mississippi River, he brought with a well-earned reputation for great daring and physical courage—a reputation he successfully upheld until stricken down by the assassin McCall at Deadwood, in June, 1876. But it was not of Wild Bill I started to write, but of one whose daring exploits on the frontier will not suffer by comparison.

The purpose of this article is to tell a story of Bill Tilghman, who was among the first white men to locate a buffalo-hunting camp on the extreme southwestern border of Barbour County, Kansas, just across the Indian Reservation line, as far back as 1870. Billy Tilghman is one of the few surviving white men who reached the south-west border of Kansas before the advent of railroads, who is still in harness and to all intents and purpose as good both physically and mentally as ever.

It is now thirty-seven years since a slim-built, bright-looking youth, scarcely seventeen years old, pulled up for camp one evening on the bank of the Medicine Lodge River in southwestern Kansas, only a few miles north of the boundary line between Kansas and the Indian Territory. An Indian uprising lasting more than a year had been put down the year previous by General Custer, and, as a natural consequence, the Indians who had taken part in the uprising entertained for the white man anything but a friendly feeling.

Billy Tilghman, like others in that country at the time, became a buffalo hunter and was working along nicely until the Indians got after him. The Indians, by the terms of the treaty lately concluded with the government, had no right to leave their reservation without first obtaining permission from their agent. It was therefore as unlawful for an Indian to be found in Kansas without government permission, as it would have been for a white man to enter the Indian Territory for the purpose of either hunting or trading whiskey with the Indians. The Indians, however, cared little for treaty stipulations at the time and often crossed over into Kansas for the purpose of pillage as well as killing buffalo.

The Indian, besides destroying the hunter's buffalo hides and carrying away his provisions and blankets while he was temporarily away attending to the day's hunting on the range, was often known to have added murder to his numerous other crimes, so that an Indian off his Reservation got to be viewed with apprehension by the hunters. It was a well understood thing among the buffalo hunters whose camps were located close to the Reservation line, that any time a hunter could be taken unawares by the Indians he was almost sure to be killed, if for no other reason than to secure his gun and belt of cartridges. The Indians had, in prowling around the country one day, come upon Billy Tilghman's camp, and, after cutting up what hides he had staked out on the ground for drying purposes, proceeded to set afire to those already dried and piled up ready for market.

When Tilghman and his two companions returned to camp that evening, after their day's work on the range, they found their camp a complete wreck. Besides the destruction of several hundred dollars' worth of hides, they also found that the noble red men who had paid their camp a visit during their absence had carried off everything there was to eat. But, as buffalo hunters found no trouble in making a hearty meal on buffalo meat alone, they did not despair nor go to bed on an empty stomach.

The day's hunt had resulted in the taking of twenty-five buffalo hides, and the question now arose what was to be done with them. If they were staked out to dry as the others had been, there was no reason for believing the Indians would not return and destroy them as they had the others. Tilghman's two partners were for moving away the first thing in the morning.

"We are liable to all be killed," said one of them, "if we stay here any longer."

"I think we ought to go about twenty miles farther north over on Mule Creek," said the other. "Besides the hunting is as good there as it is here, and the Indians hardly ever get that far away from the Reservation."

"We will move away from here," said Billy Tilghman in his characteristically deliberate manner, "after I get even with those red thieves for the damage they have done us."

Billy Tilghman, although a mere boy at the time, was the master-mind of that camp, and what he said was law.

"Ed," said Billy to one of the partners, "go and hitch up the team and drive to Griffin's Ranch and get a sack of flour, some coffee and sugar and a sack of grain for the horses and get back here before daylight in the morning, and Henry and I will unload those hides and peg them out to dry. Don't forget to feed the team when you get there and let them rest up for an hour or two, as you will have plenty of time to do that and get back here by daybreak."

Griffin's Ranch was fifteen miles north of Tilghman's camp on the Medicine Lodge River and the only place nearer than Wichita, which was one hundred and fifty miles farther east, where hunting supplies and provisions could be obtained.

Ed was soon on his way to Griffin's Ranch, which only took about three hours to reach. While Tilghman and Henry were busily engaged in fleshing and staking out the green hides, Billy remarked that if those thieving Cheyennes came again around his camp for the purpose of destroying things, there would likely be a big pow-wow take place among the Indians as soon as the news of what occurred reached them, "for," said he with some emphasis, "I don't intend to stop shooting as long as there is one of them in sight."

"But supposing," said Henry, "that there is a dozen or so of them when they come, what then?"

"Kill the entire outfit," replied Billy, "if they don't run away."

There was little else said on the subject before bed-time, but as Henry afterwards told me, it was not a hard matter to understand by Tilghman's actions that the only thing that seemed to worry him was the fear that the Indians would fail to pay the camp another visit.

Before daylight the following morning, Ed was back in camp, having carried out his instructions to the letter. After breakfast that morning, Tilghman informed Ed and Henry that they would have to hunt without him that day, as he intended to conceal himself nearby the camp, so as to be in a position to extend a cordial welcome to the pillaging red-skins when they showed up. Billy, as a precaution, planted himself before the other boys left for the hunting ground, so that in case the camp was being watched by the Indians, they could not tell but what they had all left camp as they had done the previous day. About noon, and just as Billy was commencing to despair, one lone Indian made his appearance. He rode up very leisurely to the top of a little knoll where he could get a good view of the camp, and, after a careful survey of the surroundings, and discovering nothing to cause alarm, proceeded to make the usual Indian signals, which is done by circling the pony around in different ways. Tilghman, who was crouched down in his little cache, was intently watching the Indian, understanding as well as the red-skin did, the meaning of the pony's gyrations. Directly six other Indians rode up alongside of the first and proceeded to carefully make a mental note of everything in sight.

They soon concluded that there was no lurking danger and all rode down to the camp and dismounted. This was exactly what Billy had been hoping they would finally conclude to do. Now if they will only all dismount, said Billy to himself, as he saw the Indians riding down to camp, I will kill the last one in the outfit before they can remount. He got his wish, for they all hopped off as soon as camp was reached. Billy, however, waited for awhile to see if they intended mischief, before opening up on them with his Sharp's big fifty buffalo gun that burned 120 grains of powder every time it exploded a shell. He did not have long to wait, for no sooner had one big buck hit the ground than he ran over to the sack of flour and picked it up and threw it across his pony's back, while some of the others started out, as Billy supposed, to cut up the freshly staked hides.

The big Indian who had swiped the sack of flour had scarcely turned around before Tilghman dropped him in his tracks with his rifle. This, as might be supposed, caused a panic among the other Indians, who little suspected that there was an enemy nearer than the hunting ground, until they heard the crack of the gun. In an instant Billy had in another cartridge, and another thieving Cheyenne was sent to the happy hunting-ground. The first Indian that succeeded in reaching his pony had no sooner mounted him than he was knocked off by another bullet from Billy's big fifty. This made three out of the original seven already killed, and what was an unusual thing for a Southern Plains Indian to do, the remaining four abandoned their ponies and took it on the run

Bill Tilghman (photo courtesy Western History Department, Denver Public Library).

61

for a nearby clump of timber, which all but one reached in safety. Billy managed to nail one more of the fleeing marauders before he could reach the sheltering protection of the woods. The shooting attracted the attention of his partners, who were not more than two miles away, causing them to hurry to camp, where they expected to have to take a hand in a fight with Indians, whom they had reason to believe were responsible for the shooting they had heard.

"The scrap is over," said Billy, when the boys got near enough to hear him, "and three of the hounds have made their escape. I told you last night, didn't I, Henry, that I would kill all that came if they stood their ground and didn't run away. Well," he said, in a rather disconsolate tone of voice, "I fell down somewhat on my calculations, as seven came and I only succeeded in getting four, but then that wasn't so bad, considering that they left us their ponies."

"What's to be done now?" inquired Henry, who was not hankering for a run in with the Indians at that time.

"Don't get frightened," said Billy; "and remember that we are in Kansas and that those dead Indians were nothing more than thieving outlaws who had no right off their reservation and if any more of them come around before we are ready to leave, we will start right in killing them."

There was nevertheless little time wasted in getting away from that locality. The camp dunnage was loaded into the wagon in a hurry, and the team headed towards the north, and Ed, who was driving, told to keep up a lively trot whenever possible. Billy brought up the rear mounted on one of the Indian ponies and driving the others.

"Look here, Billy," said Henry, as they were about to pull out of camp, "don't you think we ought to bury those dead Indians before leaving?"

"Never mind those dead Indians," replied Tilghman, "the buzzards will attend to their funeral; go ahead."

When dark overtook the party that night they were on Mule Creek, twenty-five miles from where they had pulled up camp at noon. The Indians reported the occurrence of the killing to their agent at the Cheyenne Agency, but received no satisfaction, and were informed that they were liable to be killed every time they left their reservation without permission.

That was Tilghman's first mix-up with the Indians, but it was not his last. He continued to hunt in that country, and as the Indians persisted in crossing over into Kansas, there were many clashes between them, which invariably resulted in the Indians getting the worst of the encounter.

A Scout for the Government

During the fall and winter of 1873-4, there was practically no cessation of hostilities between the Indians and hunters along the Indian border, finally culminating in an uprising among the four big southern tribes, namely the Cheyennes, Arapahoes, Kiowas and Commanches, which required almost a year for the government to put down. In this Indian war of 1874, Tilghman acted as a scout for the government and several times while carrying dispatches from one commander to another, had to fight his way out of mighty tight places with the Indians in order to save himself from being taken alive. After the Indian uprising had been put down, Tilghman went up on the Arkansas River and took up a ranch close to Dodge City, where he lived for several years. In 1884 he was appointed City Marshal of Dodge City, and made one of the most efficient marshals the city every had. He was just the sort of a man to run a town such as Dodge City was in those days, being cool-headed, courageous and possessing excellent executive ability.

In the summer of 1888, a County-seat war broke out in one of the northern tier of counties in the state of Kansas, and Tilghman was sent for by one of the interested parties to come up there and try and straighten the matter out. Tilghman went and took with him a young fellow by the name of Ed Prather, whom he had every reason to believe he could rely upon in case of an emergency. Prather, however, proved to be a traitor, and one day attempted to assassinate Tilghman, but the latter was too quick for him, and Prather was buried the next day. After straightening out the County-seat trouble, Billy returned to Dodge and continued to live there until the opening up of Oklahoma Territory, fifteen years ago.

He was among the first to reach the territory, and took up a claim at Chandler, Lincoln County, where he still resides. Tilghman acted as U.S. Deputy Marshal when he first went to Oklahoma and did as much if not more to stamp out outlawry in the territory as any other man who ever held office in that country.

The Capture of Bill Doolin

Tilghman has served four years as Sheriff of Lincoln County, and during that time has killed, captured and driven from the country a greater number of criminals than any other official in Oklahoma or the Indian Territory. His capture of Bill Doolin in a bath-house at Eureka Springs, Arkansas, single-handed, was perhaps the nerviest act of his official career. Doolin was known to be the most desperate criminal ever domiciled in the Indian Territory and had succeeded for several years in eluding capture. A large reward was offered for his apprehension and a number of U.S. Marshals with their deputies had several times attempted to arrest him, dead or alive, but in every instance Doolin either eluded them or, when too closely pressed, stood them off with his Winchester. Doolin was credited with the killing of several Deputy Marshals. Tilghman got after him and trailed him to Eureka Springs where he found him in a bath-house, and without calling on the local officials for assistance, effected his capture single-handed. Doolin was seated on a lounge in the bath-house when Tilghman entered, and before the desperado realized what was happening, he was covered by a 45-calibre Colt's pistol and ordered to throw up his hands. Doolin hesitated about obeying the order and Tilghman was forced to walk right up to him and threaten to shoot his head off unless he instantly surrendered. Doolin had his pistol inside his vest and directly under his armpit, and made several attempts to get it before he was finally disarmed. It was certainly a daring piece of work on the part of Tilghman, and he was lucky to get away with the job without being killed.

Bill Raidler was another notorious outlaw whom Tilghman got after, but in this case the Marshal was forced to kill his man before he could take him. Tilghman and Raidler met in the road in the Osage Indian Country, and Tilghman ordered the outlaw to throw up his hands, but instead of obeying he opened fire on the Marshal, who instantly poured a fistful of buckshot into the desperado's breast, killing him in his tracks. Raidler had been a pal of Doolin's and had been mixed up in several train robberies and had sent word to the U.S. Marshals that if they wanted him to come and get him, but to be sure and come shooting. Tilghman was too good a shot for him at the critical moment and Bill Raidler's life paid the penalty for his many crimes.

Thomas Calhoun, a negro, was another notorious outlaw and murderer whom Marshal Tilghman captured in the Territory, but not until after he had shot and broken the desperado's leg did he succeed in making him a prisoner. Calhoun was charged with the murder of a colored woman and a warrant for his arrest placed in Marshal Tilghman's hands. The Marshal came upon Calhoun and ordered him to throw up his hands, which he refused to do, and promptly opened fire on Tilghman, who, as he had so often done before, returned it with such good effect that the negro's leg was broken and he then surrendered, but died soon afterwards.

Dick West, known as "Little Dick," was perhaps the worst criminal in the entire territory outside of Bill Doolin. "Little Dick" was a member of the Doolin gang of train robbers, and the hardest outlaw in the Territory to trap. He never slept in the house, winter or summer, and kept continually changing about from one place to another. Tilghman finally got track of him and ran him to cover, when a fight ensued. Tilghman, though shot at several times, escaped without injury and finally succeeded in killing his quarry.

"Little Dick," like his chief, Bill Doolin, had for several years made a specialty of ambushing and murdering U.S. Deputy Marshals in Oklahoma and the Indian Territory, and when the announcement of his death at the hands of Deputy Marshal Tilghman was made, there was universal rejoicing among the law-abiding citizens of that country. Space forbids that I go further into the career of William M. Tilghman at this time. It would take a volume the size of an encyclopedia to record the many and daring exploits and adventures of this remarkable man. His life's history has been aptly stated by a magazine writer as almost a continuation of the memoirs of Davy Crocket or the story of Kit Carson, as far as it relates to his adventures on the frontier of Kansas in the early seventies. After a career covering a period of thirty-seven years, spent mostly on the firing-line along civilization's lurid edge and after being shot at perhaps a hundred different times by the most deperate outlaws in the land, men whose unerring aim with either gun or pistol seldom failed to bring down their victims, this man Tilghman comes through it all without as much as a scratch from a bullet.

Sheriff for More than Thirty Years

Billy Tilghman was born in Iowa in 1854, and moved to Atchison, Kansas, in 1856, and as a boy, passed through the reign of terror known in that country in those days as the Kansas and Missouri border war, which existed for a number of years along the frontier of those two states. It was a fierce and bitter contest between the pro-slavery influence of Missouri on the one side and the abolitionists of Kansas on the other, which finally culminated in the Civil War.

At the time Alton B. Parker received the democratic nomination for the presidency in 1904, Billy Tilghman was selected by the Democratic National Convention as one of the delegates to notify Mr. Parker of his nomination, and was last in New York at that time. He is still a resident of Chandler, Lincoln County, Oklahoma and will in all probability be elected Sheriff again there this fall. He is perhaps the only frontiersman living who has been almost constantly on the job for more than a generation, and who still lives on to tell the story.

"Billy" Tilghman
Well-known as buffalo hunter, Indian fighter and
government officer on the western frontier in the seventies

THE SPECIAL AGENT'S WORK.

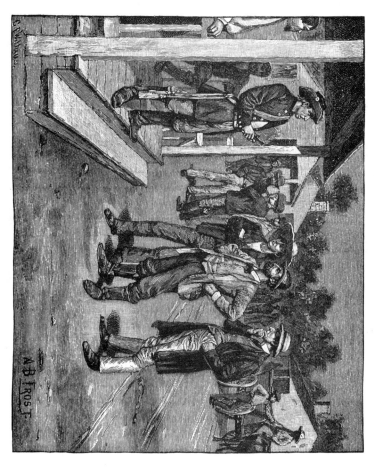

THE CHALLENGE.

BUFFALO BILL ON HORSEBACK.

FROM THE FAMOUS PAINTING BY ROSA BONHEUR.

Get there first and dont Miss

W F Cody

"Buffalo Bill"

Famous Gun Fighters of the Western Frontier

Colonel Cody

Hunter, Scout, Indian Fighter

A Few Incidents in the Adventurous Career of the Famous "Buffalo Bill" That Have Passed Under My Personal Observation. His Early Days on the Western Frontier.

by W. B. (Bat) Masterson

The Colonel Ready to Enter the Ring
From a recent photograph

It almost seems like profanation at this late day to assert that Col. William F. Cody was not the original Buffalo Bill. Such, however, is the case. That distinction belongs to William Mathewson, known by his friends for more than a generation before his death, as "Old Bill Mathewson." The original Buffalo Bill kept a ranch and stage station on the old Santa Fe trail at the crossing of the Little Arkansas River near where now stands the town of Halstead, Kansas, during the Civil War, and was known to both the White and Red men of that region, as Buffalo Bill. It is altogether likely that he himself never knew why or when he first came by the name. Cody who has since made the name famous from Manitoba to Moscow and from the Gulf of Mexico to the Nile, was at that time, a mere boy, living in the Salt Creek Valley, a short distance above Leavenworth, on the Kansas side of the Missouri River.

Cody's family moved from Iowa to Kansas while the latter was yet a territory, and settled on a farm in the Salt Creek Valley, outside of Leavenworth. It was at the time when the question of whether slavery should or should not be introduced into Kansas when it became a state. It was along the Kansas and Missouri border where the prelude to the mighty tragedy of the Civil War was first enacted, and the Cody family found itself well up on the firing line. The settlers of Kansas were arrayed against those of Missouri. It was free soil against slavery with no quarter as the motto. Kansas and free soil finally won the battle, but not without a long and bitter struggle in which much good red blood was shed on both sides. In such an atmosphere and among such scenes, young Cody passed a number of his boyhood years.

It was not my purpose, however, to attempt a biography of Colonel Cody, the world-famed Buffalo Bill of to-day. I will leave such an undertaking to more capable hands and endeavor to interest my readers by relating a few incidents in the career of the famous hunter, scout, Indian fighter and showman which have passed under my own personal observation. Colonel Cody got the name of Buffalo Bill during the time the Kansas Pacific railroad was being built through Western Kansas. About the year 1867, the road had been built as far West as Hays City and Cody took a contract to furnish buffalo meat at so much per month. He was at that time the finest specimen of young manhood in the West. Standing full six feet, as straight as an arrow, strong as a lion and as quick and nimble as a cat. His hair was long and as black as that of an Indian. He was an expert horseman and could shoot a pistol with deadly accuracy, while riding his horse at full speed.

Pistol in Both Hands, Reins in Teeth.
Cody, in those days, used pistols altogether in killing buffalo. He would ride his horse full tilt into a herd of buffalo and with a pistol in either hand and the bridle reins between his teeth, was almost sure to bring down the day's supply of meat in the first run. With six shots in each pistol, he often killed as many as eight buffalo on a run. This feat was never equalled, although many times attempted by men who fancied they could ride and shoot as well as Cody. Although the country fairly warmed with desperate men during those years when Buffalo Bill was making history in the West, it is not on record that he ever engaged in a deadly duel with a white man. This was perhaps due to the fact that he had never been called upon for such a purpose. That he would fight if his had was forced was no secret among those who knew him best.

He had been known on more than one occasion to take a swaggering bully by the neck and after relieving him of his lethal decorations soundly shake him until he promised to behave himself. During the several Indian wars which have occurred in different parts of the West in the last forty years, Cody, as scout and guide, has rendered valuable service to the government. He has taken a more or less active part

70

in every expedition the government has sent against the hostile red man since the war of 1868, and by his unerring knowledge of the country and by the skill and fidelity with which he carried out every duty assigned to him, earned for himself a reputation among the army officers who commanded those expeditions second to no man who ever filled a like position.

Such veteran Indian fighters as General Carr, Custer, Royal, Crook, Miles, Merritt and numerous others, equally celebrated in Indian warfare, have testified to the undaunted courage, thorough reliability and great powers of endurance so often displayed by Buffalo Bill while leading the united States soldiers against the red savages. The value to the commander of an Indian expedition of a competent and thoroughly reliable guide can not be overestimated. Thje services of such a man are absolutely indispensable. The safety and success of the command rests almost entirely on the knowledge and reliability of the guide.

General Richard Irving Dodge correctly states the case in his thirty years among wild Indians. Besides mere personal bravery says General Dodge, a scout must possess the moral qualities associated with a good captain of a ship, full of self-reliance in his own ability to meet and overcome any unlooked for difficulties, be a thorough student of nature, a self-taught weather prophet, a geologist by experience, an astronomer by necessity, a naturalist and thoroughly educated in the warfare, stratagems, trickery and skill of his implacable Indian foe. Because in handling expeditions or leading troops, on him alone depends correctness of destination, avoidance of dangers, protection against sudden storms, the finding of game, grass, wood and water, the lack of which of course is more fatal than the deadly bullet. In fact more lives have been lost on the plains from incompetent guides than ever the Sioux or Pawnees destroyed.

With the possible exception of Ben Clark, Buffalo Bill typifies those qualities better than any man who has ever acted as scout or guide against the Indians in the West. Ben Clark has been a scout, guide and Indian interpreter for the Government for the last fifty years, and is still on the job at Fort Reno, Indian Territory. Although he has been a leading figure in all the Indian outbreaks which have taken place throughout the West since the breaking out of the Civil War, and has, through force of circumstances, on numerous occasions been thrown in contact with all manner of desperate and lawless characters, he has never been known to have had a serious run in with a white man. Like buffalo Bill, he has repeatedly fought and killed the red warrior but has managed somehow during all these years to live in peace and harmony with the pale face.

Buffalo Bill has been a showman for the last thirty-five years and during that time has presented in a genuinely realistic manner not only to the people of his own country, but to those of foreign lands, scenes and incidents in the daily life or the pioneers of our once boundless frontier.

Colonel Cody has made North Platte, Nebraska, his home for a generation or more, and owns in conjunction with Major North, one of the finest horse and cattle ranches in the state. In the summer of 1880, I had occasion to go from Dodge City,

Residence of Hon. W. F. Cody (Buffalo Bill) at North Platte, Neb.

Buffalo Bill Cody driving a phaeton
(photo courtesy Western History Department, Denver Public Library)

Kansas, where I was Sheriff, to Ogallalla, Nebraska, which is about sixty miles West of the little town of North Plate, on the Union Pacific Railroad. My object in going to Ogallalla at the time, was to straighten out, if possible, a serious difficulty in which a personal friend of mine, by the name of Billy Thompson, a brother of the famous Ben Thompson of Texas, had become involved with a local man by the name of Bill Tucker, which resulted in Thompson being severely wounded by Tucker, and the latter having the thumb and fingers of his left hand shot away by a bullet from Thompson's pistol, during the melee. Ogallalla was a mere hamlet at the time, there being not more than thirty buildings in the place. Tucker kept a saloon in which the game of Spanish Monte was dealt for the cattle men and cow boys who worked on the range near by. Being a local man, Tucker had the home sentiment with him in his fight with Thompson.

When I arrived in Ogalallalla, I found Thompson laid up in bed in the hotel from the effects of the several wounds he had received from Tucker. I also found him under arrest with a Deuputy Sheriff guarding him in his room. After talking the matter over for a while with my wounded friend, I concluded with a view of bringing about an amicable understanding between the warriors, to go and see Tucker, whom I also found in bed at his home with his left hand minus thumb and fingers done up in liniment soaked bandages. Although Tucker was mostly to blame for the trouble, I found him very bitter against Thompson. I also found, before I had proceeded far afield, that he was willing to listen to reason if the proper inducements were offered. The sum, however, was beyond the reach of Thompson or his friends, therefore my conference with the thumbless one was soon at an end. I returned to my friend's room and told him of the failure of my mission and together, we commenced to formulate another plan of action. As a primary step, it was decided that Thompson should make out to be suffering greatly all the time and whenever he felt like changing his position in bed in order to rest more comfortably to be sure and call upon the guard to assist him.

Perfecting a Plan of Escape

As there were no doctors in Ogallalla in those days, the extent of Thompson's injuries could not very well be scientifically determined so, by playing a clever part, he could make them appear much more serious than they really were. My purpose in having Thompson play such a part, was to keep him from being put in jail which I learned the local authorities purposed doing as soon as he was considered sufficiently recovered to be moved. My next move was to get on friendly terms with the guard, who was a young fellow who had lately reached that country from one of the New England states. His armament consisted of a long barrelled Colts, 45 caliber pistol with a white handle of which he seemed duly proud. Although Thompson was not as badly injured as he let on to be, he had nevertheless been sufficiently crippled to be of little use to himself in case of an emergency. I had decided to get Thompson out of the country in some way but couldn't make up my mind how to go about it. Had Thompson been able to ride a horse, it would have been easy for us to escape in that manner but that was out of the question. If, on the other hand, we attempted to escape by wagon, we would be easily trailed and overtaken by the posse we knew would soon be in hot pursuit. There was therefore but one avenue of escape left for us, and that was by railroad. But how we were to be able to reach the train without being detected, was a problem that involved much serious thought on our part. We figured that if we could reach North Platte where Buffalo Bill was living, we would have better than an even chance in making our escape from the country. The East bound overland flyer reached Ogallalla about midnight and stopped long enough to fill its tank with water and then sped on to North Platte, its first stop.

But how to get by the guard and get Thompson, who was unable to walk, on board the train, was anything but an easy task for me to perform. It seemed as if everybody in town was watching every move I made, and from what I subsequently heard, I am satisfied they were. I had no sooner arrived in town than the Sheriff, thinking perhaps that I might make an attempt to rescued his prisoner, issued the strictest kind of instructions to his Deputy who had been assigned to guard Thompson, to never leave the room for a moment while he was on duty and I can truthfully say he obeyed the instructions to the very letter. One Sunday night, however, there was a dance given by the people of the town and as was the custom in those small Western hamlets in those days, everybody in the place attended the blow-out. The dance was given in the shoolhouse which was also used for church purposes whenever a preacher happened along that way. The building,, which wasn't much larger than a good sized hen-coop, was situated on a little knoll about four hundred yards north of the depot which was located in the centre of the town. The Sheriff, who was also the town fiddler, was furnishing the music for the occasion and, as was to be expected, nearly everybody in Ogallalla was at the dance. Jim Dunn was the name of the bartender in the hotel where Thompson was being guarded. He was a Texan and an artist in his business. He had previously tended bar in Dodge City and we were the best of friends. This was obviously my time for getting away with Thompson. If Jim the bartender would assist me a little, there was nothing to it. Thompson and I would be in North Platte before the fiddling Sheriff would realize that we were gone.

We Get Away on the Overland Flyer
I hunted up Jim and explained what I wanted. "Leave it to me," said Jim. I then went up to Thompson's room and, as the weather was war, the windows were raised, furnishing us a splendid view of the doings at the schoolhouse. "I am sorry I'm not at the dance," I remarked to the Deputy, "for they seem to be having a good time up there." "They are certainly enjoying themselves," replied the Deputy. "What say you about having a drink," I said, "just to even up on the dance." "Very well," said he, "I don't mind if I do." I stepped to the head of the stairs and called to the bartender, who instantly responded. "What will it be, gentleman," inquired Mr. Dunn, as he entered the room. "Bring me a sour whiskey," I said. "That will do me," said the Deputy. "Nothing for me," said Thompson. In a few minutes Jim was back with the drinks. "Mine tasted fine,"—"so did mine," vouchsafed the Deputy. In a little while the order was repeated and we drank to our natural good health. Soon after the Deputy disposed of the second drink, he spread himself on the floor and was soon dreaming of his New England home. I then proceeded to dress Thompson as hurriedly as circumstances would permit, and when I saw the train coming, I got him on my back and carried him downstairs and over to the depot and got him aboard the train before it had hardly come to a stop. In a few minutes we were speeding at the rate of forty miles an hour for North Platte, where we arrived about two o'clock in the morning. When the train pulled up at the station, I again put Thompson on my back and carried him out on the platform. After being informed by one of the station

hands which direction to go, in order reach Dave Perry's saloon, I again picked up my burden and lit out along the dark street and was soon inside the saloon, where I found Buffalo Bill and a dozen others all having a good time. As a matter of course, we were given a royal welcome and were immediately taken in charge by Colonel Cody, who found a safe place for us to remain until he could outfit us for the trip across the country to Dodge City, which was about two hundred and fifty miles South from there.

General Sheridan's Party of Foreigners

"The Ogallalla authorities will not take you from here," said Cody to us that night, and we slept quite comfortably. The next day I went up to Colonel Cody's home, a beautiful place in the suburbs of North Platte, and found him busily engaged in raising a flag pole in honor of General Hancock, who had just been nominated by the Democratic party for President of the United States. I may here state that Buffalo Bill is a Democrat, but that should not be held against him, for he is a splendid fellow, and perhaps regrets it as much as any genuine American could. The next day Cody gave us a fine big Texas horse, and his wife's phaeton to carry us across the country, home.

About this time, General Sheridan had sent out to North Platte a party of distinguished foreigners who had come to this country for the purpose of travelling through the West. General Sheridan requested Buffalo Bill to take charge of the party and show then what there was on the plains that he thought would be of interest. Twenty-five miles south of North Platte, a man by the name of Keith owned an immense cattle ranch, on which he had a small herd of tame buffalo and, as this ranch was on our way home, Buffalo Bill and his party of distinguished foreigners accompanies us that far. There were fully twenty persons in the party, and as everybody was feeling good, when we left North Platte the trip to Keith's was a right royal one, you may be sure. I was driving a double team hitched to Cody's specially made mess wagon, which was loaded down with everything imaginable. There were all sorts of large wooden boxes filled with different kinds of ammunition and a photographer's outfit, which Cody had brought along for the purpose of photographing his foreign guests as they stood among the tame buffalo at Keith's ranch. The caravan would stop every little while and liquor up, and then go on until the next liquoring-up point was reached, when the caravan would again come to a halt. Cody, who had been riding alongside of me for a while, finally concluded to take a nap and stretched himself out full length on top of the load of dunnage in the mess wagon. We had gone only a short distance after Bill had fallen asleep when the wagon was tipped completely upside down. I was pitched out on my head in the prairie while Cody was actually buried underneath the wagon and its contents. I gathered myself up as quickly as I could, and got hold of the horses by the head and held them until other members of the party came and rescued Cody, who had not received as much as a scratch, while I had my lower lip nearly torn from my face.

The Colonel's Wife Loses a Phaeton

We reached Keith's in due time without further mishap, and what a time those foreign gentlemen were given that night after the supper table had been cleared away. Buffalo Bill was then in his prime, and the stunts he did with pistol and rifle and in horse-back riding, were nothing short of wonderful. When Cody got back home to North Platte, his wife asked him what had become of her fine phaeton and harness. I don't know exactly what he told her or how he accounted for their disappearance, but he afterwards told me that a much more expensive outfit soon replaced the one he had given us.

The day Thompson and I left Keith's ranch for Dodge City, a heavy rainstorm set in which lasted during the entire trip and, as we had nothing but the sky for a roof, our appearance can better be imagined than described, when our destination was reached. About the first thing Thompson did after reaching Dodge was to send a telegram to the Ogallalla Sheriff notifying him of his safe arrival and inviting him to come and get him in case he still thought he wanted him. The fiddling Sheriff made no reply to Thompson's message, and there the matter ended.

As He Looked in 1873
From a hitherto unpublished photograph

Editor's acknowledgment: This article on Colonel Cody has not appeared in earlier editions of "Famous Gunfighters of the Western Frontier." It was located at the Knight Library of the University of Oregon by Philip J. Panum of Denver Public Library's Western History Department and thereby made available for the present edition.

COL. W. F. CODY
"BUFFALO BILL"

Published by A. Hoen & Company.

THE MAGIC OF THE "DROP."

The King of the Gun Players

William Barclay Masterson

by Alfred Henry Lewis
editor of Human Life Magazine

Mr. Masterson in 1907.

WILLIAM Barclay Masterson was born in Iroquois County, Illinois, about fifty-three years ago. His father was a farmer and came originally from St. Lawrence County, New York. His mother and father still live, and count themselves among the Sedgewick County pioneers of Kansas, with a sunflower residence that reaches rearward half a century.

First a Kansas farm boy, Mr. Masterson — subject of this memoir — was early abroad upon the plains. What is farm land now was savage wilderness then, and those who invaded it did so with a knowledge that their hands must keep their heads. For twenty years, beginning when he was thirteen, Mr. Masterson lived by his own personal powers of offense and defense, and was in more or less daily peril of death from Indians, or from outlaw spirits—common enough, these latter, in the West of that hour.

Has Wasted Least Lead of any Man

Just as some folk are born poets, so others are born shots, and Mr. Masterson from the first evinced a genius for firearms. With either rifle or pistol he proved himself infallible, and of all who ever pulled trigger he has wasted least lead. It was as a hunter he won his name of ''Bat,'' which descended to him as it were from Baptiste Brown, or ''Old Bat,'' whose fame as a mighty Nimrod was flung all across, from the Missouri River to the Spanish Peaks, and filled with admiration that generation of plainsmen which immediately preceded Mr. Masterson upon the Western stage.

INDIANS ON THE WAR-PATH.

80

For his deadly accuracy with the rifle, Mr. Masterson was early employed to "do the killing" for great hunting outfits, which in the '70's ransacked the country between the Arkansas and Canadian, for buffaloes in the name of robes and leather. Mr. Masterson would "kill" for a dozen men to skin and cure; and the majestic character of that commerce, wherein he bore his powder-burning part, may be guessed at from the fact that, in such years as 1872, more than three hundred thousand buffalo hides, to say naught of one-fourth as many robes, were shipped eastward from the single town of Dodge.

Crossing and re-crossing the buffalo ranges, Mr. Masterson came naturally by a close knowledge of the country, and, in a region not overstocked of water, could locate every spring and stream, as surely as astronomers locate stars. Thus it befell that General Miles was quick to enlist him as scout, in his campaigns against the Cheyennes in '74. In truth there were more than the Cheyennes engaged in that trouble; for those copper-colored Richards drew with them to the field the flower of the Kiowa, Comanche and Arrapaho tribes.

It is to be thought that Mr. Masterson himself was, in half fashion, the partial first victim of that war. The cunning Indians were—apparently—steeping themselves in peace, with never a notion of warpaths and paleface scalps. They were none the less sedulously, and not always quietly, about the collection of what rifles and pistols and cartridges they could lay red hands upon. Mr. Masterson was one day skinning a buffalo he had killed, when a quintette of Cheyenne bucks rode amiably up. They belonged with old Bear Shield's band, whose home-camp was on the Medicine Lodge. Mr. Masterson thought little or nothing of the five Cheyennes. They were every-day sights in his life, and the last thing he looked for was trouble. He kept on with his skinning, merely ejaculating "How!" to clear himself of any imputation of impoliteness.

Mr. Masterson's rifle was lying on the grass—a 50-caliber Sharp's buffalo gun, for which he had paid eighty dollars. One of the Cheyennes carelessly picked up the rifle, as though to examine it. As he did so, another reached across—Mr. Masterson was bending over the dead buffalo bull, skinning knife in hand—and whipped the six-shooter from the Masterson belt. At these maneuvers Mr. Masterson straightened up, and was just in time to receive a confusing blow over the head from his own rifle. The 8-square barrel cut a handsome gash, and covered his face with blood. As the Cheyenne struck the blow, he broke into excellent agency English, through which flowed a dominating element of profanity, and commanded Mr. Masterson to "dig out."

Since the Cheyenne had the muzzle of the rifle not two feet from his stomach, and those four fellow Cheyennes evinced an eagerness to bear a helping hand, Mr. Masterson decided to "dig out." That is to say, with blood covering his face he backed away from the rifle-pointing profane Cheyenne, towards a ravine which yawned conveniently in his rear. Arriving at the brink, Mr. Masterson with hasty strategy fell into that saving canyon, and was out of range in a moment.

Running along the bottom of the ravine for half a mile, Mr. Masterson reached his own buffalo camp. After a consultation with his two camp mates, the whole party packed their burros, and pointed their noses for Dodge, sixty miles to the north. Mr. Masterson, sore of head from the blow and sore of heart from the loss of his new rifle, was all for following the five Cheyennes and giving them battle. But his comrades, whose unvisited heads were still intact, and whose hearts had been wrung by no rifle losses, overruled him. They said, "Let's pull our freight," and they pulled it.

DISSOLUTE COW-PUNCHERS

Mr. Masterson, however, was not to be consoled. That night—Christmas night it was—he rode back, and ran off forty of old Bear Shield's ponies. These brought him twelve hundred dollars in Dodge, and repaired what monetary losses he had suffered, to say the least. The wounds to his head, and to his honor, *vide licet* his boyish vanity, which those five Cheyennes had inflicted, he cured later at the battle of the 'Dobe Walls.

It was in the last days of June that the fight at the 'Dobe Walls occurred. The "'Dobe Walls" consisted of two buildings, one a great outfitting store belonging to Mr. Wright, present head of the Kansas State historical society, and the other Mr. Hanrahan's saloon. The latter gentleman is now, I think, a member of the Idaho legislature; but, at the time whereof I write, he cheerfully conducted a bar and restaurant, for the comfort of what buffalo hunters worked along the Canadian, two hundred miles south of the last sign of civilization.

There were fourteen buffalo hunters at the 'Dobe Walls that night in June. Nine—among them Mr. Masterson—slept in Mr. Hanrahan's saloon, and five in Mr. Wright's store. Not one anticipated attack.

Luckily, about three o'clock in the morning, the roof—a dirt roof—of Mr. Hanrahan's saloon fell in. The sleeping buffalo hunters were forced to turn out. This was all that saved them; otherwise the prophecy of the Comanche medicine man would have been fulfilled, and the buffalo hunters knocked on the head as they slumbered.

Morning came streaking the east, and found the buffalo hunters still engaged in aiding Mr. Hanrahan about the restoration of his roof. It was at this moment of morning that full five hundred Indians, the picked warriors of the Kiowas, Comanches, Arrapahos, and Cheyennes, swung out from the shadow of a fringe of cottonwoods that ranked the Canadian river.

In a moment, every buffalo-hunting man jack of them, abandoning roof for rifle, clawed up his gun and took to a window. Mr. Masterson's window mate was Mr. Dixon, who has since—for the sentiment of the thing, perhaps—homesteaded the one hundred and sixty acres which include the 'Dobe Walls, and makes the same his residence.

The Famous 'Dobe Walls Battle

The firing instantly began, and the charging Indians had the tremendous worst of it. The Indian is in several respects defective. He is a bad shot; he won't dismount and fight on foot; and he is so much the Parthian that it's against his religion to fight in the night. Mr. Masterson and his fellow buffalo-killers were, in these three particulars, the precise opposite of their enemies. They were dead shots; they preferred to fight on foot; and, as for night and day, when it came to bloodshed the two were synonymous. Daylight or dark, they transacted their wars the moment the foe was found, holding—as held a famous jurist concerning the law—fighting to be a so sacred matter that "for it all places are palaces, all seasons summer." Wherefore, when those hopeful five hundred savages charged, the fourteen hunters tore into them blithely with their big buffalo guns, and began emptying redskin saddles at a most disheartening rate. The Indians charged fiercely three times, and the unerring

Mr. Masterson and his friends corded up over twenty of them. The siege, before all was over, lasted two weeks; but the fighting, so far as the Indians were concerned, after those first three furious charges—which broke the aboriginal teeth—was but half-hearted and desultory.

To tell the whole of the battle at the 'Dobe Walls, would go beyond the limits of an article such as this. The excited comments of a tame crow which, while the fight raged, flew chatteringly to and fro from Hanrahan's to Wright's and back again, would of themselves make a story; while how Mr. Masterson crossed to Wright's store in quest of cartridges for a pet rifle he possessed, and was deeply bombarded *in transitu* by a wounded Kiowa hiding in a clump of weeds; how a boy in Wright's died from a bullet in his lungs; how Old Man Richards walked through a hail of lead to a pump ten rods away in the open, and, while a dog was killed at his feet, and his hat shot from his gray head, and bullets plowed and spattered the pump platform and ground about him, drew a bucket of cool water for the dying boy; how a wild tenderfoot, one Thompson—killed afterward by Billy the Kid—persisted, in the teeth of command and the very face of slaughter, in rushing forth to rob dead Indians of their war bonnets and guns; how the lookout on Hanrahan's roof blew out his own brains instead of an Indian's; how Mr. Masterson, in the plenitude of his young conceit, leaped from a window and scalped a Comanche—he owned an unusually alluring top-knot, black and glossy—under the very noses of his scandalized tribesmen; how each night the beleagured ones, to save their own noses, must bury the dead Indians and ponies; how throughout the long two weeks, when not at the windows fighting, the said beleagured ones beguiled the tedium of their lives by profound games of draw poker, how the Comanche medicine man was luckily killed by Mr. Masterson on the first charge; how that same faultless rifle shot afterward brought down a negro bugler, who had deserted the standards of Uncle Sam for those of the Cheyennes, and was then sounding charge and rally as war music cheering to the aboriginal heart; and how finally, after two weeks, the cavalry came down from Dodge and raised the siege, must one and all, as battle elements, wait for their relation upon occasion more comprehensive than this. Suffice it that the Indians were beaten, with a whole battle-loss—by their own story told later at the agencies—of over eighty killed, to the meager count of one slain by savage lead on the side of the buffalo hunters.

His First Gun Trouble

Once, so runs the tale, a gentleman of extensive pistol practice was testifying as a witness. "How many men have you killed?" asked the cross-examining lawyer.

The witness seemed for the moment posed, almost puzzled. At last, as one seeking exact light, he enquired:

"You don't mean Mexicans and Indians?"

The cross-examining lawyer explained that he intended only white men, Mexicans and Indians to be excluded. The witness then took up the count.

Excluding Mexicans and Indians, Mr. Masterson's first gun trouble was at Mobeetie in the Texas Panhandle, the theatre thereof being a dance hall called the Lady Gay. Sergeant King, a soldier and a gambler, found fault with Mr. Masterson, and lay in prudent wait to take his life at a side door of the Lady Gay.

The evening was dark. A girl named Anna Brennan came up. The lurking King, giving some excuse, asked her to rap at the door, conjecturing that Mr. Masterson, who was just inside, would open it. The King conjecture was justified; Mr. Masterson did open it, and asked the girl what was wanted. At the sound of his voice, King stepped forward and, placing the muzzle of his pistol against the Masterson groin, fired. King fired a second shot, and accidentally killed the girl. Coincident with that second shot, however, Mr. Masterson's pistol exploded, and King fell shot through the heart. The girl, King and Mr. Masterson went down in a bleeding heap; the two first were buried, while to the amazement of the surgeons at Fort Elliot, Mr. Masterson was back in the saddle by the end of eight weeks. So much for the recuperative powers of one who had lived healthfully and close to the ground.

Mr. Masterson's hat measures seven and three-eighths. Wise, cool, wary, he is the born captain of men. Generous to a final dollar, the poor and needy make for him like night birds for a lighthouse. To a courage that is proof, he adds a genius for justice, and carries honesty to the pitch of romanticism. To these virtues of mind and heart, add the thews of a grizzly bear, and you will have a picture of Mr. Masterson. Such he is; such he was when, at the age of twenty-two, the public elected him sheriff for Ford County, whereof the seat of justice was the stormy little city of Dodge.

Smothering Ebullient Cow-Boys

As sheriff, Mr. Masterson's duties carried him over sixteen unorganized counties, besides the county of Ford. His more immediate reponsibility, however, was the good order of Dodge, and to prevent ebullient cow-boys, when the Autumn herds came up, from ''standing'' that baby hamlet ''on its head.'' It took judgment and nerve and forbearance and military skill; but Mr. Masterson accomplished the miracle, and did it, too, at a minimum of bloodshed. In the words of a satisfied citizen and taxpayer:

''He never downed a man who didn't need it, and kept Dodge as steady as a church.''

Scores of lurid spirits, whose lives were forfeit by every Western rule, have been spared to live a quieter life by the forebearing Mr. Masterson. Mr. Sutton, a lawyer and a present resident of Dodge, was out recently in the papers with a story in illustrative point. Three cow-boys, moved of whisky and a taste for violence, dashed down the single street of Dodge, their six-shooters blazing like roman candles. Most peace officers would have harvested these boys; Mr. Masterson was more leniently inclined, since thus far the young merrymakers had not succeeded in hitting anybody. Sure of its aim, Mr. Masterson's pistol barked three times. Two of the ponies fell, and Mr. Masterson dragged their riders—sprawled all abroad in the dust of the street—off to the calaboose.

The third pony lasted until he reached the south side of the Arkansas, and then dropped dead. Thereupon, its rider stripped off saddle and bridle, ''stuck up'' the incoming buckboard, and compelled the driver to turn nose-about, and land him at a nearest ranch more than forty miles away.

There was a lady aboard the buckboard who sang in the theatres. She was coming north from Mobeetie to fill a Dodge engagement. As shortening those tiresome forty miles, the dismounted cow-boy—pistol in hand, eye on the buckboard driver who might at any moment rebel—told the cantatrice that he thought she ought to sing. With that she thought so too; and so for forty miles she warbled ''Silver Threads Among the Gold,'' and kindred melodies of concert hall vogue at the time. This boy got clear away, while the ravens and the coyotes, at their feast over his dead pony, gloried in the fatal accuracy of the Masterson guns.

As demonstrating his huge strength, Mr. Masterson once seized a recalcitrant cow puncher who, seated in his saddle, was making ready to ''shake up the village.'' The cow-boy was himself as strong as whalebone, and gripped his pony with legs of iron. Throwing his soul into the business, Mr. Masterson gave that adhesive cow-boy such a wrench—the boy meanwhile clinging to his mount like grim death—that both pony and boy were thrown heavily to the ground.

It was not always convenient, nor even feasible, to spare the blood of the wrong doer. The following might furnish an example in line. Mr. Kennedy rode up to the Alhambra, kept by Mr. Kelly, the then Mayor, and took a shot

Mr. Masterson in 1888. Taken in Denver

at that publican and magistrate with his Ballard. Mr. Kennedy missed Mr. Kelly, and killed a lady who had come to the Alhambra to have part in the nightly ball. Mr. Kennedy—it was eight o'clock in the evening—on the heels of the homicide, dug spurs into his pony's flanks, and flew southward through the darkness. He was heading for the Canadian two hundred miles away.

Mr. Masterson saddled a fleetest horse, and started 'cross country for the ford where the flying Mr. Kennedy must cross the Medicine Lodge. There were three or four trails, and direct pursuit in the dark was out of the question. Mr. Masterson reached the ford in the gray of the morning, bettering Mr. Kennedy's time by an hour. He hobbled his horse, and threw himself in behind a convenient knoll, to wait the coming of the murderous flying one. At last the latter drew near, eye scanning the ribbon of trail to the rear, pony worn and panting. No wonder, this last; seventy miles, at a swinging hand gallop, is no mere canter.

"Hold up your hands!" cried Mr. Masterson.

Mr. Kennedy almost leaped from the saddle with the surprise of it; he wasn't looking for an enemy in front. The next moment, however, he pulled himself together, and drove a bullet at Mr. Masterson from the Ballard. Mr. Masterson was quite as brisk. The retort of his big buffalo gun made one report with the Ballard; Mr. Kennedy's shot went wide, while the 50-caliber bullet from the buffalo gun tore its fearful way into his side. As he fell, an accidental yank on the Spanish bits brought the tired, broken pony with him.

Mr. Kennedy rolled a dying eye upon Mr. Masterson.

"You blankety-blank-blank!" said Mr. Kennedy; "you'd ought to have made a better shot than that!"

"Well, you blankety-blank murderer!" quoth Mr. Masterson, "I did the best I could."

Mr. Masterson's brother Ed was made Marshal of Dodge, somewhat against the wish of Mr. Masterson. The latter feared that the "bad men," who came and went in Dodge, would "out manage" his brother, whose suspicions were too easily set at rest.

The Killing of Mr. Masterson's Brother

It fell out as Mr. Masterson had feared. Mr. Wagner, drunk and warlike, sought to enter Mr. Peacock's dance hall, questing trouble. Marshal Ed Masterson, instead of pulling his own gun, as prudence would have dictated, and stopping the violent Mr. Wagner with the cold muzzle thereof, seized that truculent person by the shoulders. Instantly, Mr. Wagner's six-shooter was brought to the fore. With that, Marshal Ed Masterson shifted his left hand to Mr. Wagner's wrist, and for the moment put that drunkard's weapon out of commission. There the two stood, the situation dead-locked.

From across the street, Mr. Masterson saw events and started to his brother's aid. He was still sixty feet away when Mr. Walker, who, like Mr. Wagner was a person of cows, ran from the dance hall, and snapped his six-shooter in Marshal Ed Masterson's face. The cartridge failed to explode. Mr. Walker was never given the chance of trying a second; for Mr. Masterson put three bullets from his Colt's 45 through him before he could hit the ground. As the dead Mr. Walker went down, Mr. Wagner, still in a grapple with Marshal Ed Masterson, got his gun to bear, and shot Marshal Ed Masterson in the body. The latter fell wounded to the death, coat afire from the other's powder. Mr. Wagner fell across him, a bullet from Mr. Masterson's pistol through his brain.

And after this fashion did Mr. Masterson maintain law and order in Dodge. Many were his battles, many the wounds he wrought; and it was said that the local doctor traced half his practice to the untiring efforts of Mr. Masterson in behalf of communal peace.

Once upon a time in Dodge a general war was missed by narrowest margin. Those dead worthies, Messrs. King, Kennedy, Wagner and Walker had come one and all from Texas in their day, and Lone Star feeling, always clannish, seldom nicely critical, resented their taking off. It is not too much to say that ten thousand dollars might have been borrowed on Mr. Masterson's scalp in a dozen Texas towns. Scores of stark souls came north with the herds, avowing no other intention than to wipe out the hated Mr. Masterson.

Among these was Mr. Driscol—big, violent, formidable. Mr. Driscoll was not in Dodge ten minutes before Mr. Masterson introduced himself.

"I'll give you half an hour," said Mr. Masterson, "to put yourself the other side of the Arkansaw; and if you ever jingle a spur in Dodge again I'll shoot you in two."

Mr. Driscoll crossed the "Arkansaw"; and later—his laurels somewhat tarnished, and not caring to return to Texas under such diminished circumstances—he journeyed down to Springer, and went to work for Senator Dorsey's "Triangle-dot."

Mr. Burlison was Sheriff of Colfax County, New Mexico, where the Dorsey ranches were, and Mr. Masterson wrote his brother officer a letter.

"Dear Burlison," said Mr. Masterson, "this man Driscoll, who has migrated to your neck of woods, will bear watching. He's a four-flush and a bully. If he tries to start anything down your way, go right at him and he'll quit."

Mr. Driscoll "started" something. Mr. Burlison went "right at him," and Mr. Driscoll "quit." Also when he "quit" he was dead.

Mr. Allison was a Texan by adoption, and a friend of Mr. Driscoll. Likewise, he was lame with a club-foot, limped when off his horse, and used a Winchester for a crutch. He had slain many men, and took a quiet pride in the fact that, in the teeth of local ordinances to the contrary, he never took his guns off when he visited any town.

"Kill Every Man with a Big Hat"

Mr. Allison was in Dodge when Mr. Masterson introduced himself to the offensive Mr. Driscoll. Being coldly advised, however, by Mr. Masterson, Mr. Allison was not wearing his hardware. In the day that followed the banishment of Mr. Driscoll, the whisper went the Dodgian rounds that the

Texas cow people, then and there in large numbers, were making war medicine, and would presently "turn loose" under the leadership of Mr. Allison. With that the careful Mr. Masterson made preparations; and such berserks as Mr. Earp, Mr. Brown, Mr. Kelly, Mr. Holiday, Mr. Bassett, Mr. Short, and others whose names were high and famous in the annals of that hour, began cleaning responsive shotguns to be in readiness for the Masterson call to arms. The word was, if war broke out, to "kill every man with a big cow hat on." The Dodgians, be it known, wore hats of moderate and exemplary rim.

Mr. Masterson believed that if carnage descended it would come in the night. Which perhaps was the reason why Mr. Allison chose the afternoon. Of a sudden, the latter gentleman rode into the middle of that single thoroughfare—so often a battlefield— armed to the teeth. Halting his horse in front of Mr. Webster's Alamo, Mr. Allison spake loud and fiercely, but he was heedful to leave Winchester and pistols in their scabbards, and, while his oratory was terrible, his hands continued as harmlessly empty as a child's.

Mr. Masterson at the time was sitting in his office. With the earliest note of war from Mr. Allison, he snatched up a shotgun and "covered" that Texas chieftain. Since Mr. Masterson was to the rear of Mr. Allison, the latter enthusiast did not notice his "covered" condition.

Having Mr. Allison "covered," Mr. Masterson turned to Judge Colborn, now of Salt Lake City, then District Attorney of Dodge.

"Skip out the back door, Judge," observed Mr. Masterson, "and tell Wyatt and the rest that I've got Allison dead to rights. Tell them not to close in on him; if he reaches for a gun, I'll hive him. When they hear me shoot, let them get busy right and left; tell them to bump off every Texan they find in the town."

The warning word went down the line, and Mr. Allison was left unmolested in his eloquence. But that very fact made him uneasy. He was not without a working knowledge of homicide as a science; and the sight of the several heads of Messrs. Earp and Holiday and Bassett and Short and a score besides protruded in an expectant fringe from doors and windows all along the street, as though a common idea obtained that something interesting was about to happen, chilled him and bid him pause. Mr. Allison looked excessively bothered. Finally he shut down his oratory in mid flow, got off his horse, limped dubiously into Mr. Webster's Alamo saloon, and took a thoughtful drink. Mr. Masterson put away the shotgun and joined him. Observing Mr. Masterson enter, Mr. Allison pretended great joy.

"Where were you, Bat?" he asked. "I've been looking all over town for you."

"I've been see-sawing on you with a shotgun for ten minutes," returned Mr. Masterson grimly, "What's the matter, Clay?"

Mr. Allison appeared a bit confused, but explained that he had been aroused by the insults of a red-headed hardware clerk who didn't know who he, Mr. Allison, was. Being calmer now, he would again disarm in deference to the prevailing local taste as to shooting irons.

Thus the business passed without actual hostilities, and Mr. Allison confessed later that his reason for "simmering" was he had had a "premonition." It's just possible he did. In any event, and whatever the cause, his change of offensive front that afternoon saved many a life. Also, it saved Dodge from what would else have proved the ruddiest chapter in all her crimson history.

"Had It In" for "Bat"

When the new liquor law took effect in Kansas in '81, Mr. Masterson laid down his office. He was not sumptuary, and, while he himself never drank liquor, refused to be drawn into deadly collison with gentlemen whose only offense had been a too vehement thirst. Besides, he urged, considering the many strenuous years he had gone through, he felt he had earned a rest.

There was at least one gentleman in Dodge who didn't share this vacation view. The hour was evening, and Mr. Masterson, no longer sheriff, was sitting in the rear room of Mr. Kelly's Alhambra, in talk with Judge Colburn. Mr. Bell appeared abruptly in the door, a six-shooter in his right hand, another in his belt. Mr. Bell is the sober, quiet sheriff now of that same county of Ford; but in these, his younger years, he was a sturdy customer, and had "shot up" several of his acquaintances. Per incident, he "had it in" for Mr. Masterson.

"I think," remarked Mr. Bell, as he stood thus triumphantly in the door— "I think there's a horned toad here I want to kill."

Like a flash, the sensitive Mr. Masterson—who, had he been either slow or dull would never have lived till now—was on his feet, the muzzle that never missed pointing squarely between the eyes of Mr. Bell. Naturally, the latter warrior froze up; he stood as though planet-struck.

There was a darkling pause; then Mr. Masterson, gun still unwaveringly upon Mr. Bell, began slowly to advance. Mr. Bell never moved. Coming within reach, Mr. Masterson suddenly let down the hammer of his pistol and smote Mr. Bell such a jealous blow upon the head that he went to the floor, and from the floor to his bed for two weeks.

Years later, I asked Mr. Masterson why he withheld his fire. "I didn't think I had to shoot," he said. I once saw Bell jump over a bar-counter to get at a man, when he might just as well have gone round, and it struck me all at once that he was much too dramatic. If it had been Wyatt Earp now, or Doc Holiday, or Luke Short, or Ben Thompson, I'd have begun to bombard him out of hand. But I didn't think such extreme measures were demanded in the case of Bell;" and here Mr. Masterson smiled peacefully at the retrospect. "My size-up of Bell may have been wrong," he concluded, "and if it was I hope he'll pardon me. He ought to; for, between us, it was all that saved him from death that day."

Some of his Other Adventures

This chronicle of Mr. Masterson might be extended to one hundred thousand words, and only the half be glanced at, not told. I might relate how he rescued from a mob the State's Attorney General, and the Chief of the Prohibition Leagues of Kansas, when those reforming functionaries led a temperance crusade against Dodge. Or how, when Mr. Webster of the Alamo and incidentally Mayor of Dodge, exiled Mr. Short of the Long Branch—the rival shop—Mr. Masterson, then a citizen of Leadville, returned to Dodge at the militant head of such choice fighting men as Wyatt Earp, Doc Holiday, Henry Brown, Shotgun Collins, and Shoot-your-eye-out Jack, to say naught of the redoubtable Mr. Short himself, and restored that persecuted one to all his property right, as well as what elevated station, as owner of the Long Branch, he should occupy in the social life of the place. Or how—this was a case of mistaken identity—Mr. Masterson smote the Pueblo railway policeman so grievously upon his skull with a six-shooter, that the latter officer, who had wrongfully assailed Mr. Masterson with a bludgeon, must be furloughed to a hospital for a month. Or how Mr. Masterson took a man from a mob of lynchers at Buena Vista, and carried him before a magistrate; and how, when the magistrate, in sympathetic league with the lynchers, would have committed the man to the local jail, where the mob could get at him, he, Mr. Masterson, tore up the commitment papers in the face of the court, and carried the man off to the Denver jail, where subsequently he was sufficiently yet lawfully hanged. Or how Mr. Masterson protected Mr. Holiday from the requisition of Arizona's Governor for killing Mr. Stillwell in Tucson, by the simple strategem of having that consumptive gun player put under arrest on a charge of highway robbery — a fiction — in Colorado. Or how, when Mr. O'Neal, with a six-shooter in each overcoat pocket, and a hand on each six-shooter, sent forward a drunken ruffian to attack Mr. Masterson, with full and fell intent on Mr. O'Neal's part of "bumping off" Mr. Masterson when once entangled with the drunken one he, Mr. Masterson, knocked the drunken one senseless with his left fist, while with his right hand he abruptly acquired the drop on the designing Mr. O'Neal. With that never-erring six-shooter upon him, Mr. O'Neal's empty hands came out of his pockets, and went into the air, like winking.

"Don't kill me!" he faltered.

Mr. Masterson's finger was itching upon the trigger. In an instant he shifted. Letting down the hammer, he repeated the maneuver which had worked so well in the days of Mr. Bell. Later, the wounded Mr. O'Neal, head in bandages, sent from his bed a message of peace, asking Mr. Masterson to see him, and give him an opportunity to "explain."

"Well," said Mr. Masterson to the messenger, "I'll come. But tell O'Neal to be careful, and keep his hands outside the blankets while he's doing his 'explaining.'"

Or I might set forth how a dear but intoxicated friend, forgetting for the moment—an election moment wherein the "dear friend" resented the indomitable republicanism of Mr. Masterson—those close social ties which subsisted between them, pulled his pistol, intending the destruction of Mr. Masterson; and how Mr. Masterson shot the weapon from his dear friend's hand, and let him live to apologize for his murderous rudeness. That apologetic one is sober now, and a Denver detective of much good repute.

Or I could tell how Mr. Gallagher of Denver imported a desperate character, one Smith, for the wiping out of Mr. Masterson; and how Mr. Masterson,

Mr. Masterson in 1878
He was then Sheriff of Ford County, Kansas

when he heard, sent a 100-dollar bill to Mr. Gallagher, with word that the money was his if he would but walk down the street "as far as Murphy's," with his importation. Also, how Mr. Gallagher refused the money, and how Mr. Smith made haste to explain that his purpose in coming to Denver was wholly innocuous.

Or how—if these be not enough—Mr. Masterson journeyed, in the name of friendship, to far-off Ogallala, and surreptitiously bore away Mr. Thompson—then under arrest, but stiff and sore from buckshot wounds, and held captive in a hotel instead of the jail, because of them. Mr. Masterson, having advantage of a drunken sentinel, rolled the injured Mr. Thompson in a blanket, and packed him to the station on his shoulder, Mr. Thompson aiding his rescue by conveniently fainting away. It was two o'clock of a dark morning, every Ogallalan was at a dance in the far end of camp, and no one beheld the feat. Which was just as well, since there were more buckshot in Ogallala than had been stopped by Mr. Thompson. Mr. Masterson carried Mr. Thompson aboard train as far as North Platt; and there the excellent "Buffalo Bill" Cody presented the fugitives with his wife's phaeton, and a horse of a temper like Satan's and a hideous hammer head, with which double donation they made their safe way cross-country three hundred miles to Dodge.

Now Out of the Zone of Fire

Or I might give the story of how, when Mr. Short killed Mr. Courtright in Fort Worth, Mr. Masterson took his six-shooters and begged the privilege of sitting in Mr. Short's cell all night, fearing mob violence. Friendship such as Jonathan's would have hesitated at so desperate a step! It turned out well, however, for the would-be lynchers, told by the Sheriff that Mr. Masterson and Mr. Short were together in the jail, and each with a brace of guns, virtuously resolved that the law should take its course, and went heedfully home to bed.

These and many more have been the adventures of Mr. Masterson, who, coming up through all this perilous trail of smoke and blood, is now peacefully amassing ten thousand dollars a year, as crack writer on a New York City paper and a contributor to *HUMAN LIFE*. I asked him if he never yearned for the West. He shook his head.

"I'm out of that zone of fire," said he, "and I never want to go back. I hope never to see those dreary plains again."

But the plains come to Mr. Masterson on Broadway, or rather the men of the plains. One day he introduced me to a wiry, eagle-eyed gentleman, dressed as though just out of a bandbox.

"Mr. Tighlman," said the introductory Mr. Masterson.

Mr. Tighlman, it appeared, was East as the democratic representative of Oklahoma, to notify Mr. Parker that he had been nominated for the Presidency.

"Do you remember," Mr. Masterson asked — "do you remember my telling how, one Christmas eve, I ran off forty of old Bear Shield's ponies? And how I saw a party riding about among the herd that I took to be an Indian herder? It was Billy here; he got away with something like fifty good head himself that night."

Mr. Tighlman—now a sheriff in Oklahoma—beamed at the rich suggestion of those aforetime ponies, and then he and Mr. Masterson fell to remembering how Mr. Masterson had one day given Mr. Tighlman warning at Leota to "look out for Ed Prather;" and how the next afternoon Mr. Tighlman "looked out" so earnestly that Mr. Prather departed headlong into the misty beyond.

"Billy kept the tail of his eye on him," explained Mr. Masterson; "and when Ed reached for his gun, he beat him to it."

One last adventure, and I am through. Mr. Masterson had not seen Dodge for a handful of years. He was in Deming when a telegram was put into his hands. It related to his younger brother, who was still in Dodge. It ran:

"Come at once. Updegraffe and Peacock are going to kill Jim."

Mr. Masterson was thirty hours reaching Dodge. Unable to sleep, his fancy roved feverishly ahead and drew dark pictures of the probable. Mr. Updegraffe was as game a man as ever buckled a belt, and Mr. Peacock would fight a little. By the time Mr. Masterson reached Albuquerque, he knew that Jim was dead; and when he had got as far as Las Vegas, he felt sure that the funeral was over. In this frame he stepped off the cars at Dodge next day. There they were; Mr. Updegraffe and Mr. Peacock, waiting for him in the little public square.

Mr. Masterson cut short suspense.

"You murderers," he cried to the waiting Updegraffe and Peacock, "might better begin to fight right now!"

"For Shooting Inside of City Limits"

Mr. Updegraffe's bullet buried itself in the side of a Pullman. Mr. Masterson's bullet drove a 5-inch splinter of rib through Mr. Updegraffe's lungs. Mr. Peacock took refuge behind the calaboose, from which coign he fired wild and high, breaking four-story windows in a far-away block. Mr. Masterson shot twice at Mr. Peacock, and missed him by a breath. The scars of those two bullets still show on the side of Dodge's calaboose. Mr. Masterson, aiming to dislodge him, charged the entrenched Mr. Peacock. When he arrived at the corner of the calaboose, Mr. Peacock had vanished. Mr. Masterson caught a disappointing glimpse of him, as he disappeared into Mr. Gallon's hotel.

At this pinch, Mr. Webster—Mayor, propietor of the Alamo and no friend of Mr. Masterson—came panting up, a 10-gauge shotgun in his shaking hands. Mr. Masterson who never forgot his strategy, went instantly and close to Mr. Webster. Mr. Webster was visibly shaken, and as white as paper. Mr. Masterson surveyed him—eye keen as that of a lynx, six shooter in ready hand.

"What's the matter with you, Web?" asked Mr. Masterson.

"It's just this, Bat," stammered Mr. Webster. "I'm Mayor of this outfit; and this shooting's got to stop."

"Well," returned Mr. Masterson, as steady as a tree, "I think it has stopped, unless you choose to start it again."

"I'll not start it," ejaculated the fervent Mr. Webster.

"Then let me take the 10-gauge," said Mr. Masterson, soothingly, at the same time claiming that weapon. "It doesn't look well for the Mayor of Dodge to be running about the streets with a shotgun in his hands."

Then the unexpected happened. Jim Masterson, not at all dead and buried, but clothed and in his right mind, came running up. Mr. Masterson stared as though he beheld a ghost.

"Where have you been?" he gasped.

"Over in the Wright House, asleep," returned Jim, "until your cannonading woke me up."

There had been trouble with Messrs. Updegraffe and Peacock on one end of it and Jim on the other. Some shooting had taken place, but no one scored. While the brothers stood talking, Mr. Peacock as closing the incident, sent forth an ambassador who paid Jim six hundred dollars—the *casus belli*.

"Get your blankets," Mr. Masterson said to Jim. "Out of town you go by the next train! I've had to come twelve hundred miles on your account, to kill one of my friends, and now I won't even let you stay in the State. Get your blankets; you and I take the next train west!"

"But, Bat," expostulated Mr. Webster tremulously, "I've got to have you arrested."

"Be careful, Web!" warned Mr. Masterson. "I won't submit to an arrest. Your people here took to shooting at me the moment I got off the cars; I only defended myself. I give you warning that any one who attempts to arrest me will have to arrest me in the smoke."

"Not for downing Updegraffe," protested Mr. Webster hastily; "that, as you say, was self-defense. But, Bat, we've passed some ordinances since you were here—ordinances ag'inst shootin' inside the town." This last tentatively.

Mr. Masterson smiled: "To ease your official mind, Web," he said at last, "so it's nothing more than a money fine, and you don't over-size my pile, I'll stand it."

Thereupon, Mr. Webster, Mayor, cheered up mightily, and fined **Mr.** Masterson five dollars for "Shooting inside the city limits"; which sum Mr. Masterson tossed to Mr. Webster, who as Mayor, gratefully collected it off the grass.

A PROHIBITORY LAW.

HOLDING UP A TREASURE COACH IN THE BITTER CREEK COUNTRY.